ANUPAMA CHANDRASEKHAR

Anupama Chandrasekhar is a playwright and former journalist
based in Chennai, India. She was the National Theatre's first
international playwright-in-residence and a Charles Wallace India
Trust Writing Fellow at the University of Chichester. Her plays
have been translated into several languages and staged at leading
venues in India, Europe and the US. Among her works are *Free
Outgoing* and *Disconnect*, both of which premiered at the Royal
Court Theatre in London, and *When the Crows Visit*, which
opened at the Kiln Theatre. She was a runner-up for the London
Evening Standard Award for Most Promising Playwright and a
finalist for the Whiting Award (UK), and the Susan Smith
Blackburn Prize (US) for *Free Outgoing*. Her screenplay
adaptation of the play was a finalist for the Sundance
International Screenwriters' Lab, Utah. Her short story *The Wings
Of Vedanthangal* was the Asian winner of the Commonwealth
Short Story Competition. Her other plays include *The Snow
Queen* (Unicorn Theatre/Trestle Theatre/UK and India tour); *Acid*
(QTP, Mumbai/Madras Players, Chennai) and *Closer Apart*
(Theatre Nisha, Chennai). Short plays include *Kabaddi-Kabaddi*
(Royal Court Theatre – International Human Rights Watch Film
Festival); *Whiteout* (Royal Court Theatre, BBC Radio World
Drama) and *Anytime, Anywhere* (Theatre Kimaayaa).

Other Titles in this Series

Anupama Chandrasekhar

THE FATHER AND THE ASSASSIN

NICK HERN BOOKS

London

www.nickhernbooks.co.uk

A Nick Hern Book

The Father and the Assassin first published as a paperback original in Great Britain in 2022 by Nick Hern Books Limited, The Glasshouse, 49a Goldhawk Road, London W12 8QP

The Father and the Assassin copyright © 2022 Anupama Chandrasekhar

Anupama Chandrasekhar has asserted her right to be identified as the author of this work

Cover image: Photography by Simon Sorted; background artwork photography by Prarthna Singh
Art direction by National Theatre Graphic Design Studio

Designed and typeset by Nick Hern Books, London
Printed in Great Britain by Mimeo Ltd, Huntingdon, Cambridgeshire PE29 6XX

A CIP catalogue record for this book is available from the British Library

ISBN   978 1 83904 071 9

The Father and the Assassin was first performed in the Olivier auditorium of the National Theatre, London, on 19 May 2022 (previews from 12 May). The cast was as follows:

VINAYAK SAVARKAR	Sagar Arya
MADHAV/KISHORE	Ankur Bahl
MOHANDAS GANDHI	Paul Bazely
AAI	Ayesha Dharker
PANDIT JAWAHARLAL NEHRU	Marc Elliott
SARADAR VALLABHAI PATEL	Ravin J Ganatra
VIMALA	Dinita Gohil
MOHAMMAD ALI JINNAH	Irvine Iqbal
MITHUN	Nadeem Islam
BABA	Tony Jayawardena
NARAYAN APTE	Sid Sagar
NATHURAM GODSE	Shubham Saraf
DAULAT/BRITISH POLICEMAN	Peter Singh
KISHEN	Maanuv Thiara
ENSEMBLE	Ralph Birtwell
	Halema Hussain
	Sakuntala Ramanee
	Anish Roy
	Akshay Shah

Director	Indhu Rubasingham
Set and Costume Designer	Rajha Shakiry
Lighting Designer	Oliver Fenwick
Movement Director	Lucy Cullingford
Composer	Siddhartha Khosla
Musical Director	David Shrubsole
Sound Designer	Alexander Caplen
Fight Directors	Rachel Bown-Williams
	and Ruth Cooper-Brown
	of Rc-Annie Ltd
Dialect Coach	Shereen Ibrahim
Company Voice Work	Jeannette Nelson
Staff Director	Gitika Buttoo
Dramaturg	Emily McLaughlin

For my beloved Amma,
my best friend and moral compass

Acknowledgements

Special thanks to my grandmother and my father whose stories about Gandhi and India's past spurred this play.

My debt to Rufus Norris, Clint Dyer, Ben Power, Dominic Cooke, Nina Steiger and the wonderful New Work Department, for their support and encouragement at all stages. The residency at the Studio gave me invaluable time, space and inspiration to read, watch, learn and write. Thanks also to Lookout Point, who supported my residency.

Thanks, as always, to my good friends Anushka Ravishankar and Timeri Murari for their insight, wisdom and company.

A.C.

My deepest gratitude to my two fellow-travellers on this journey: Indhu Rubasingham and Emily McLaughlin. I could not have birthed this play without them!

Characters

NATHURAM GODSE, *seven to thirty-nine*
MOHANDAS GANDHI, *forty-eight to seventy-eight*
NARAYAN APTE, *eighteen to thirty-eight*
VIMALA, *seven to thirty-nine*
VINAYAK SAVARKAR, *forty-five to sixty-five*
SARDAR VALLABHBHAI PATEL, *forty-two to seventy-three*
PANDIT JAWAHARLAL NEHRU, *twenty-eight to fifty-nine*
MOHAMMAD ALI JINNAH, *forty-one to seventy-two*
KISHEN, *thirty, policeman/jailer*
DAULAT, *thirty, policeman /jailer*
MITHUN, *forty, school watchman*
AAI (*Mother*), *Godse's mother, twenty-eight to sixty-two*
BABA (*Father*), *Godse's father, thirty-three to sixty-five*
MADHAV, *nine*
KISHORE, *fifty-five, Indian tailor*
MAGISTRATE

And other assorted characters

Note on the Staging

Godse is on stage throughout the play.

Godse and Vimala as children and adults are played by the same actors.

Many characters age through the play, including Godse.

Characters in a crowd with speaking roles are named 1, 2, etc., for convenience and are not meant to be the same people all through the play.

Although the scenes are numbered, they're not discrete units. Rather each should bleed seamlessly into the next.

Setting

Various places across India, particularly Maharashtra (Baramathi, Ratnagiri, Pune) and Delhi.

Time

One strand of the play begins with the assassination of Gandhi on 30 January, 1948, and ends with the deaths of Godse and Apte.

A second strand of the story traces Godse's life and Gandhi's political impact from 1917 to the fateful day in 1948.

A third strand of time is now.

Note on Speech Pattern

/ denotes point of interruption.

* text indicates verbatim quote/s or based on quote/s from a speech/article.

Glossary

HINDI

Nath – nose ring

Ki jai – victory to

Satyagraha – literally, insistence on truth; form of non-violent civil resistance developed by Gandhi

Bapu (Gujarati) – Father

Kaka – Uncle

Vande Mataram (Bengali) – praise to the mother

Akhand Bharat – Undivided India

Swaraj – self-determination, self-rule

Poorna swaraj – complete independence

Ahimsa – non-violence

Himsa – violence

Hai hai – down with

Bharat Mata – Mother India

MARATHI

Aai – Mother

Baba – Father

Dada – elder brother (can be used to address older friends and strangers)

Note on the Play

This play is centred on the assassination of the Father of the Indian Nation, Mahatma Gandhi, and set against India's struggle for independence from the British Empire.

Not much is known about Gandhi's assassin, Nathuram Godse. Here's what we do know: he was born in 1910, to orthodox Marathi Brahmin parents in West India. His parents lost three baby boys in their infancy but their one girl child survived, leading them to believe that the male line was cursed. They sought a religious solution to this. They pierced Godse's nose, made him wear a nath or a nose ring and brought him up as a girl to ward off the curse. He would eventually be known as Nathuram (literally Ram of the Nose Ring). As a child, Godse was also seen as an oracle, a human channel for the Goddess Yogeshwari (another name for the Goddess Durga). He'd lose this ability well before puberty and, at some point, his family would start treating him as a boy.

Godse never went to college, having failed in English in school, and eventually became a tailor.

His father was in the postal department and was transferred frequently. While living in Ratnagiri, also in West India, Godse came into contact with the influential Hindu nationalist leader Vinayak Savarkar, who was being interned in the region.

Godse was initially a follower of Gandhi and his inclusive, non-violent struggle for Indian Independence from the British Empire, but later turned into a radical Hindu nationalist. He started a newspaper with Narayan Apte, with whom he'd plot and eventually succeed in the assassination of Gandhi. Godse and Apte were found guilty of the crime and hanged to death in 1949.

I have taken creative licence to fill in the blanks in the narrative of Godse's life. And I have used history as the frame within which to track Godse's and Gandhi's journeys, and the fatal moment of their intersection.

This text went to press before the end of rehearsals and so may differ slightly from the play as performed.

ACT ONE

1.1

Three gunshots.

NATHURAM GODSE *rises from the trap, his shirt bloody.*

GODSE (*to us*). What are you staring at? Have you never seen a murderer up close before? Take a good look. You've paid good money to be here. Do I look evil? I'm not, no matter what you've heard. I am a genuine, concerned citizen of the world who once wanted nothing more than to be a free man. To tell you the truth, you and I, we're really not that different. I'm just a bit browner than some, that's all. But I guarantee, once you get to know my story, once you truly understand me, I know you'll celebrate me. Maybe even build statues in my honour. (*To one of us.*) Oh you have a question? You'll have to wait. Teaches you to depend only on Wikipedia – or that fawning Attenborough film! With Sir Ben Kingsley. (*To us.*) It's about time you know who I am, for I too am etched in India's history.

GODSE *snaps his fingers. Cast and* RADIO ANNOUNCERS *enter.*

RADIO 1. This is All India Radio. Mahatma Gandhi was assassinated in New Delhi on the evening of January 30th, 1948 –

GODSE (*to us*). It feels like yesterday –

RADIO 2. The assassin accosted Mahatma Gandhi on the way to his evening prayer meeting and shot him thrice in the chest at point-blank range.

GODSE (*to us*). 'The assassin.' A word that gives the killer a high status because of the one he killed. Personally, I prefer the word 'murderer'. Clean, direct.

RADIO 3. The assassin has been apprehended and handed over to the police. Investigations are on to ascertain his identity –

Lights on KISHEN, DAULAT *and* VIMALA. *We are in a police station.*

KISHEN. Vimala madam, do you know him?

DAULAT. Can you identify him?

GODSE. Go on, Vimala the Weak. Tell them who I am.

VIMALA. Yes. I've known him since childhood.

GODSE. Come now, let's not exaggerate –

VIMALA. His name is Nathuram Godse. Son of retired postmaster Vinayak Godse. Editor of the Marathi newspaper *Agrani* in Pune. (*Pause.*) Your shirt. Is that…?

GODSE. Blood? Yes. – Oh it's not mine. Dried up now. It just gushed out of his chest. I didn't expect that. Didn't expect so much blood from someone who'd been on a fast unto death just ten days ago!

VIMALA. You evil butcher! What have you done? He was the father of our nation –

GODSE. Oh come off it! I did the nation a good turn – I did him a good turn! I gave him a good death! Would you rather he died of incontinence? He's a martyr now and you have me to thank for it.

KISHEN. Who planned this? Who is the mastermind?

GODSE. It was my plan, my execution, all mine – and only mine.

DAULAT. Wait a minute! (*Noting it down in his little notebook.*) Nathuram Godse. Nath, as in nose ring. Ram as in the god.

VIMALA. Yes.

KISHEN. Not a Muslim then.

VIMALA. No.

DAULAT. You are absolutely certain of this. We cannot misinform the Prime Minister of India.

VIMALA. He is a Hindu –

GODSE. A proud Hindu and a true nationalist!

(*To us*.) I am Nathuram Vinayak Godse. Journalist. Patriot. Indian. I killed Mohandas Gandhi and I have no regrets.

I've been waiting a long time for this! I can promise you a few things straight away: there's a gun in my story, a trigger is pulled, and there's blood and death – it's a potboiler!

Shall we?

(*Pause*.) But where do I begin?

AAI, GODSE's *mother, in her twenties, enters in a hurry.*

AAI. Nathu! Where are you hiding now?

GODSE (*to us*). In Baramathi, a small town in West India where drought and famine had reached our thresholds?

From another direction, MOHANDAS GANDHI *enters.*

Or in the farmlands of Champaran, in Central India, where he first thrust his vision on all of us?

GODSE *considers both options.*

Do I begin with him or with me? Is there a difference?

1.2

AAI. Gandhi who? Never heard of him!

Lights down on AAI. *We are in 1917 in Champaran, with the* FARMERS *and* GANDHI.

GODSE (*to us*). Gandhi, an Indian lawyer who'd had some success in the civil rights movement in South Africa.

Unknown here, but not for long. He's here now in
Champaran to see for himself the hellish conditions of the
farmers. He is not the first leader the desperate farmers had
invited. But he is the first who'd accepted their invitation.

FARMER 1. We are going hungry, Gandhiji. The British force
us to cultivate indigo over food crops –

FARMER 2. They force us to pay exorbitant rents for the land
we work.

FARMER 1. We pay taxes for every event of our lives – births,
deaths – weddings!

FARMER 3. We can't bear it any more!

GANDHI. This is exploitation, pure and simple. Your wedding
is your business – well, your family's too – The empire is
a leech that is sucking us dry. We need to talk to the
government.

FARMER 1. What? They're the ones who are oppressing us!

GANDHI. We cannot hope to change our destiny if we don't
engage with the government.

FARMER 2. As if they'll listen to native peasants!

GANDHI. Oh, we'll make them listen! We'll speak to all the
farmers of Champaran and collect their statements, word for
word. We'll confront the government and make our
demands.

FARMER 1. What if they arrest us?

GANDHI. Are you prepared to go to jail?

FARMERS (*hesitantly*). Yes.

GANDHI. Then I say let them arrest us. We won't retaliate.
We're going to do this in full view of the police and the
government. Without even a thought of violence.

GODSE (*to us*). In a nutshell –

GANDHI. Ahimsa.

GODSE (*to us*). Remember this word –

GANDHI. Ahimsa.

GODSE (*to us*). Translated, it means –

GANDHI. Non-violence.

GODSE (*to us*). This was the first time India heard the word in reference to a political protest. He was arrested –

GANDHI *moves to the courthouse.*

And produced in court.

1.3

MAGISTRATE. You've been charged with endangering public peace. How do you plead?

GANDHI. I plead guilty, your honour. I accept whatever punishment you wish to give me. But I'll return to the fields of Champaran the moment I'm released from jail to continue my work with these cruelly exploited farmers.

GODSE (*to us*). For a moment, do think of the poor British magistrate. A huge crowd like one you've never seen is inside the courthouse clearly on Gandhi's side. Gandhi, the silver-tongued lawyer, is defending himself. What is a judge to do? If he puts Gandhi in prison, there would be riots. If he didn't put Gandhi in prison, the British would be seen as weak.

(*To the* MAGISTRATE.) The magistrate ordered –

MAGISTRATE. Mr Gandhi, I order you to –

GODSE. No, requested –

MAGISTRATE. Mr Gandhi, I request –

GODSE. No practically begged –

MAGISTRATE. Mr Gandhi. Please pay the bail and you are free to go.

GANDHI. I won't pay bail and I won't let anyone else pay bail on my behalf either. (*Beat.*) It looks like you have no choice but to jail me.

MAGISTRATE. Right. (*Pause.*) Perhaps there's a way to compromise, Mr Gandhi. How about you don't pay bail now? Your offer of personal recognisance will do.

GANDHI. Thank you, your honour. I decline your offer.

GODSE. The move of a grandmaster! A lone Indian was standing up to our colonial rulers with no weapon at his disposal, except his wit. The whole nation was on tenterhooks: How would the magistrate rule?

Pause.

MAGISTRATE (*sighs*). I hereby dismiss the case against Mr Gandhi.

GODSE. Unbelievable! The British government cowed down. The result was –

FARMER 1 (*shell-shocked, to his friend*). Unbelievable!

FARMER 2 (*equally shell-shocked*). The government has accepted all of Gandhiji's recommendations! We can plant whatever we want.

Gandhiji ki –

FARMERS. Jai!

FARMER 2. Gandhiji ki –

FARMERS. Jai!

GODSE (*to us*). This was the moment he became our national leader… and my hero.

I was seven years old then and playing the hand I'd been dealt.

AAI. Nathu!

GODSE. Ah, I can't skirt around it any more. Look, I've not shared this part of my life with anyone before, but you seem like fair people. I'm trusting you with it. Let me try this again, from the other beginning.

AAI enters, searching for young GODSE.

1.4

1917. Baramathi, a village in Maharashtra, India.

AAI. Uff! That child will be the death of me! Where are you hiding now, Nathu?

She leaves, still looking for GODSE.

GODSE (*to us*). My mother.

Two children, a girl, seven, and a boy, nine, are hiding behind a thick, dry bush. The girl is VIMALA. GODSE, *still addressing us, puts on a nose ring.*

(*To us.*) And you've met Vimala.

The bush moves forward.

(*To us.*) No, that boy is not me. He's Madhav. (*Begins to put on a skirt.*) Let's just say I did not have a conventional childhood.

GODSE *wears a wig.*

(*To one of us, sharply.*) You have a problem? Deal with it.

He transforms into a little girl. He goes to his wooden cart and plays, as a little girl. GODSE *turns. The bush freezes.*

VIMALA. I told you there was a new girl in the village!

Has she seen us?

A moment, then GODSE *continues to play. The bush moves forward.* GODSE *instantly turns and charges towards them.*

MADHAV. Aaaah! We are under attack! Retreat! Retreat!

VIMALA. What? Wait. Why? She's just a child.

All three children crash against each other and take a tumble. GODSE *gets up and looks at them warily.*

MADHAV. What's your name?

GODSE *just watches them.*

VIMALA. What do people call you?

GODSE. Girl.

VIMALA *and* MADHAV *titter.*

VIMALA. Everyone calls me girl too.

MADHAV. Girl is a common noun.

GODSE. Aai says I'm not common. I'm special.

VIMALA *and* MADHAV *titter.*

MADHAV. Special!

VIMALA. But what is your name, the one everyone whispered in your ear when you were born?

GODSE. Nathu Godse. I'm named after my nath. (*Points to his nose ring.*)

CHILDREN. Oho! Nose-ring Godse! Nose-ring Godse!

GODSE. I can spit farther than anybody in Baramathi.

MADHAV. Oh is that so? I can spit farther than anybody in the whole Raj.

VIMALA. I can spit farther than anybody in the whole continent, in the whole world, in the whole universe.

GODSE. Prove it.

MADHAV. It's a challenge that Vimala and I, the Brilliant Bandits of Baramathi, accept.

MADHAV *draws a line on the ground with a chalk.*

This is where we'll stand. We may not step on or beyond this line. We may spit in turn. I'll mark the area where your spittle lands with these stones. Vimala goes first, I next and What's-your-name last. May the strongest spitter win. Warrior Vimala, the most fearsome female bandit ever to grace the earth, approaches the line. She bends a little, her eyes focused on the distant horizon. She clears her throat, gathers spittle from the depths of her being and she launches it like a cannonball.

MADHAV *marks the spot the spit landed.*

And it's a winner – a regional record! Will Madhav the Cunning do the impossible and beat Vimala? Will he create history in spit throwing? We shall wait and see.

MADHAV *spits. The children mark the landing spot.*

…And it's a world record. His spit has travelled thousands of furlongs against all odds to reach this… rock, this most important monument of human civilisation.

GODSE. Now, it's my turn.

GODSE *waits. When no running commentary is forthcoming:*

Aren't you going to say anything?

MADHAV. It's now the turn of the new person in the village who is named after jewellery.

VIMALA *titters.*

You may start.

GODSE *turns to* MADHAV *and spits at him and runs.*

Arrey – Catch that little rat!

The two chase GODSE.

1.5

1917. The Godse house. GODSE *is playing with his wooden train and making train noises.*

GODSE (*to us*). Before I was born, my parents had four children. Three boys – all of whom died within the first year – and a sister, who survived. So my parents believed that all the male children of their line were cursed. They made a vow to the Goddess Durga, they'd bring up the next boy they had as a girl in return for his life. (*Beat.*) I survived. No, I thrived.

AAI (*enters*). Why aren't you ready yet, darling?

GODSE (*to us*). What's more – I helped the family thrive. Because of a particular talent. (*Pause.*) Before I proceed, may I please ask you to kindly switch off your British scepticism and suspend your disbelief for a bit? Thank you. Where was I? Ah yes.

Is it time already, Aai?

AAI. Yes, darling. Now, wear this.

GODSE (*continuing to play*). Aai, I want to wear something else today.

AAI. You like this blouse.

GODSE. No I don't.

AAI. Since when? This is your only good one. We have nothing else.

GODSE *goes to the wardrobe and pulls out a shirt.*

That's Baba's. You know you can't wear those clothes.

GODSE. Why not?

AAI. They're for men. And they're too big for you. And ugly. Hold still. Would you like to wear my nose ring today? Look how beautiful it is, winking at the sun, winking at us. It's saying, 'wear me, wear me'. Do you hear it?

GODSE. Yes.

AAI removes her nose ring and puts it on GODSE. *They look into the mirror.*

AAI. See how pretty you are! It matches your skirt perfectly. You are my little miracle. Remember you are goddess touched. You are strong and clever only because of this – (*Touches his nose ring.*) and this – (*Indicates his dress.*) Now hurry up.

Pause.

GODSE. Aai? Why are there so many people?

AAI. People have heard about you, darling. They've come from all sorts of places to see you. Come on now! Don't you want to see all the gifts people have brought you? How long has it been since you ate a mango?

GODSE. Mango?

GODSE *smiles.*

BABA, GODSE's *father, in his mid-twenties, enters.*

BABA. Lakshmi! Can you hurry up? The guests are here.

AAI. We are ready!

(*In prayer mode.*) Oh Goddess Durga, we seek your guidance, we seek your answers through this child. Please accept our humble offerings.

AAI *bows her head.*

GODSE (*to us*). If I closed my eyes and focused entirely on the goddess, something would happen.

AAI. Please ask your questions. One at a time.

1. My mother is sick – Bedridden for months. Please tell me, what is wrong with her? What will cure my mother?

GODSE (*to us*). I'd get a whiff of river jasmine in the air, the fog in my head would lift and I'd hear the goddess loud and clear as the temple bell. (*To the congregation.*) Nothing.

1 (*to* BABA). What does she mean?

GODSE (*to us*). I somehow knew all the answers to their questions.

BABA. How long will her mother live, Goddess Durga?

GODSE. Two days.

1. What?

BABA. The goddess has spoken!

GODSE (*to us*). Sometimes, I knew the answers even before the questions were asked.

(*To* 2.) Yes.

2. But I haven't yet –

GODSE. Yes, your son will get married. (*To us*.) Always the marriage question!

2. That's exactly what I wanted to know! The child is extraordinary!

GODSE. But not here. Abroad. To a white woman. (*To another guest*.) Your son will pass the finals. (*To another guest*.) Yours won't.

The visitors prostrate themselves before GODSE *in devotion.*

We go to GODSE, MADHAV *and* VIMALA. MADHAV *and* VIMALA *are impressed.* GODSE *holds a mango.*

VIMALA. What does Goddess Durga look like? What does she sound like?

MADHAV. How big is she?

VIMALA. How many arms does she have?

MADHAV. Is she scary?

VIMALA. What does she feel like?

GODSE. I'm not telling you. I'm not sharing her with any of you.

GODSE *turns away from them. Lights down on the two children.*

I never actually saw her, but I heard her voice, smooth, soulful, primal and I felt her vibrations in every vein of my body. I wish I could explain just how I felt when she visited me… Imagine being high – without drugs. Being ecstatic without pills. In those moments with Goddess Durga, everything was perfect.

GANDHI *enters*.

Yet… she never once warned me about him. Why didn't she?

1.6

1917. A room. GANDHI, *forty-eight,* SARDAR VALLABHBHAI PATEL, *forty-two,* PANDIT JAWAHARLAL NEHRU, *twenty-eight, and* MOHAMMAD ALI JINNAH, *forty-one. There's camaraderie in this room.*

NEHRU. Everyone I meet is saying, 'If he can change the fate of Champaran in a few months, he can change the fate of India in a few years.'

PATEL. Your success with the farmers has certainly given us wind in our sails!

JINNAH. I am glad you returned from South Africa, Mr Gandhi. India needs people like you.

NEHRU. No, Jinnah saab. Not people like him. Him!

GANDHI. You're very kind, Nehru.

JINNAH. And very young!

Much laughter. NEHRU *takes it sportingly.*

NEHRU. Only in years, Jinnah saab. I'd love to lock horns with you at a courtroom soon. You'd perhaps change your mind then.

PATEL. I for one hope I don't meet any of you in a courtroom! I'd like to win now and then.

JINNAH. But we're not here as lawyers today, Mr Patel. We are here as Indians, because we're all fighting the same fight.

GANDHI. Which is what, exactly?

JINNAH. The British, of course.

GANDHI. We know who we are all fighting against. But what exactly are we fighting for? The end goal for which we are ready to face their gun barrels. Unless we are absolutely clear on that, we cannot take on our rulers or their system.

A brief pause as NEHRU, PATEL *and* JINNAH *contemplate this.*

NEHRU. Our survival, that's what is at stake here.

PATEL. Quite right. How can we forget the famine of '96, when over a million died across our country while the colonial government continued to export food grains? Our people are starving to death because of Britain's oppressive policies –

JINNAH. And because of the Great War! We're sending our children away to be massacred in someone else's war. We're bearing the brunt of European greed.

NEHRU. I agree. Our primary reason for existence is to keep a tiny island seven thousand miles away in luxury and security, at the cost of our own lives. I'd say this is what we're fighting for, our human rights. Our right to food, water, shelter.

PATEL. Spoken like a statesman, Nehruji. But much of our basic human needs can be met if we simply get rid of their oppressive tax regimes. I wish we could have a say in how our government is run. We need control of our own budget. For that we need representation. This is what we should be fighting for.

JINNAH. No, we should aim for more. We should be fighting for the idea of us. They've splintered us, Mr Gandhi, set Hindus against Muslims, brother against brother –

NEHRU. Divide and rule is the oldest trick in their playbook. How much more easily they're able to rule over us now!

JINNAH. Hindus and Muslims presented a united front in South Africa. That's why your Satyagraha succeeded there when all else failed. I'd like to see it replicated here.

PATEL. I concur with Jinnah saab. Lasting unity is a cause worth fighting for –

JINNAH. Or dying for.

GANDHI. As long as the British rule us, we'll be poor, hungry and divided. We will be second-class citizens in our own land.

PATEL. What do you think, Gandhiji? What should we be fighting for?

GANDHI. Independence, true and absolute.

Silence.

NEHRU. Is independence even possible?

GANDHI. Anything is possible. Whatever step we take, we don't take our eye off the bird. Long live the Motherland!

ALL. Vande Mataram!

Back in Baramathi – the CHILDREN, AAI *and* BABA:

AAI. Everyone is calling that Gandhi 'Bapu' now. 'Father.'

BABA. Do you want to see his picture?

GODSE *and* VIMALA. Yes!

BABA *shows them all a newspaper.*

VIMALA. He looks like a coolie.

MADHAV. He looks like a farmer.

BABA. He looks like a beggar.

GODSE. He looks like… (*Turns to us.*) us.

BABA *takes the newspaper, moves away from the rest and stares at* GANDHI's *picture.*

1.7

1919. GODSE *is nine years old now.* GODSE *is hiding from* BABA *and* AAI.

GODSE (*to us*). I am nine years old now and all I wanted to do, all I wanted to be was… like Gandhiji.

BABA. There you are! We've been looking everywhere for you!

GODSE (*to his parents*). I will not be coerced into doing what feels wrong and I will resist, ahimsaically.

AAI. And what are you resisting, darling?

GODSE. I don't know! But I'm on strike! Vande Mataram! (*To us.*) Our battle cry. Long live our Motherland. Vande Mataram!

AAI. Yes, yes, Vande Mataram! Now back inside! Everyone is waiting for you.

BABA (*to* AAI). Stop encouraging her obsession with Gandhi. (*To* GODSE.) Is this how a girl behaves?

GODSE. I don't want to be a girl. I hate being a girl! I want to run like the wind, I want to swim in the lake like the boys, I want to… I want to pee standing up, like you and Madhav.

Pause.

Please, Baba. I… I feel like someone has stitched me inside out. Why can't you see that?

BABA (*in low tone*). Lakshmi? Maybe it's time to speak to her –

AAI (*in low tone*). Oh no you won't. It's not yet safe for the baby.

GODSE. I just want to… be…

AAI. Be what, darling?

GODSE. I don't know! I don't want want to be this me. I want to be a different me!

AAI. You're being ridiculous now. (*To* BABA.) Tell her!

BABA. Yes. You are what you are. You are a girl and that's that. (*To* AAI.) You bring her in right away, else we'll all look like fools.

BABA *leaves. Silence.* GODSE *is upset.*

GODSE. Is something wrong with me?

AAI. Darling, of course not! Come here. You know, people say the goddess only visits girls. It's a blessing, a rare privilege. Don't you love it when Goddess Durga comes to you?

GODSE. Yes! But it's the other times, Aai, when she's not with me. I feel like, like a square peg in a round hole.

AAI. I think you are perfect as you are! Look at all the fruits people bring us! We'd go hungry otherwise. You're a good daughter, Nathu. Our golden child. Remember that!

Lights down on AAI.

Pause.

GODSE (*to us*). The answer didn't come to me in a flash, the way it did with the goddess, but slowly. Then it became clear. I ran away from home. To meet the one man who was in the business of giving hope.

1.8

GODSE. I found him on a hilltop, far away.

GODSE *runs to meet* GANDHI. *A bonfire burns. Some people have gathered.* GODSE *sits and listens to* GANDHI'*s speech.*

GANDHI. * This reign, this Raj, by foreigners need go on no longer. We can seize back our agency if we all join forces. No, not through firearms, they are the weapon of the weak.

This does not mean that we will not fight back. No, we will fight harder than those who use the bullet. Our means will be peaceful and therefore the end will be peace. Our bullet is unprofitability and will be shot straight into the heart of the British colonial rule.

The crowd murmurs.

Yes, you heard right. The Empire thrives off commerce. This is our bullseye. Remove their profitability and you remove their very reason to rule over us. So I ask you all, my brothers and sisters, boycott all goods made by oppressors.

CROWD. Yes! Yes!

GANDHI. We'll make all that we need ourselves.

GODSE. Yes!

GANDHI. Spurn foreign cloth! Burn foreign cloth! India will no longer patronise British mills.

GODSE. Yes! Yes! Burn foreign cloth!

CROWD. Burn!

GODSE. Burn!

A bonfire is being built. People burn foreign clothes.

GANDHI. We'll spin our own cloth. We'll make and wear khadi, like our ancestors used to, when we were our own people. Vande Mataram!

CROWD. Vande Mataram!

GANDHI *spots* GODSE.

GANDHI. Are you lost, daughter?

GODSE. No, Bapu.

GANDHI. Ah I see. Do you want to help then?

GODSE. Yes!

GANDHI. Go home and burn foreign-made clothes. Burn them so everyone can see.

GODSE. I'll burn them here! I'll burn them now!

GANDHI. No, my girl. Your spare clothes –

GODSE. No this! Now!

GANDHI. You are a boy.

GODSE. What?

GANDHI. You are a boy.

> GODSE *strips and burns the skirt and blouse. Stunned silence as the crowd realises* GODSE *is a boy.*
>
> *Long pause.*

GODSE. I'm… a… boy. I am a boy!

> GODSE *cowers in fear.*

GANDHI. Someone get him a kurta pyjama.

> It's alright. Don't be afraid.

> GANDHI *helps* GODSE *dress as a boy for the first time, like a father would a son. Silence.* GODSE *weeps, overwhelmed.* GANDHI *comforts him.*

> Our wars may come in many forms. On the battlefields. Within ourselves. Our goal is the truth, always. You need to find the truth in here first – (*Touches his temple.*) to fight any war out there. Ahimsa is only a weapon, the goal is always truth. Are you with me?

GODSE. I think so.

GANDHI (*laughs*). I'm sure it's all mumbo jumbo to you. Remember I expect much from you in the struggle ahead. How do you feel, my son?

> *Pause.*

GODSE. I feel… ready, Bapuji.

> GODSE *emerges as a boy.*

> (*To us.*) Do you know what truth smells like? It smells of smoke and ash. A lie, especially a lifelong one, smells like mangoes.

1.9

Back in Baramathi. GODSE *is simmering with anger.*

AAI. Where have you been? We've been… What happened to
your clothes?

GODSE. Poof!

BABA. To have a daughter run away, do you realise how much
shame you've brought to us?

AAI. We were so worried! Go change, darling. You look silly –

GODSE. No! Take a good look. This is me. This is the me
I should have been from the beginning –

BABA. Are we back to this again – (*Looking uneasily at* AAI.)
daughter?

GODSE. Son! I'm your son. From now on, this is the way I'll
dress. Why, Baba? All these years, you made me live a lie.
Why, Aai?

Answer me!

BABA. We protected you! You're alive while your three
brothers are not!

AAI (*in low tone*). We're running out of wheat again! We can't
let her do this now –

GODSE. I'm not your performing monkey, Aai! I'm your son!
You'd have me as a girl for how long, Aai?

AAI. Nathu, please, let's all –

GODSE (*aggressively*). Let's all what?

AAI (*to* BABA). Tell her –

GODSE. Him!

AAI. Him! Tell him he's a girl and she is to go to his room and
change his clothes and eat the food I've made for her, tell him.

GODSE *vents his fury on the gifts/offerings that had been
presented to him.*

BABA. Nathu! No! Stop it! You'll anger the goddess –

GODSE. You let me think I was all wrong! For this? And this?

No more of this, understand?

AAI. Nathu, no, please, stop! We're already cursed!

GODSE. I am no longer Nathu. I've chosen a name. I'm Nathuram.

BABA. Nathu... ram. We didn't do anything wrong. We only did what was best for you.

GODSE (*to us*). What would you have done? Would you have accepted their half-apology? The dutiful, pitiful Hindu son that I was, I did.

1.10

MADHAV, VIMALA *and* GODSE. GODSE *is playing by himself, studiously ignoring the other two*.

MADHAV. You look strange without a skirt.

GODSE. Do I care?

VIMALA. I think your new hair suits you.

GODSE *ignores* VIMALA.

MADHAV. I've a question. Can people just decide these things? I mean, you just decided you wanted to be a boy? How does it work?

GODSE. I am a boy.

MADHAV. And before, when you were a girl?

GODSE. I was a boy even then – I've always been a boy, and that's good because I can now fight for independence.

VIMALA. I'm going to fight for independence too, as a girl.

Pause.

MADHAV. This is all very… strange.

VIMALA. Okay let's play.

GODSE. I only play with boys. And only boy games. Like cricket. And wrestling. And boxing. Girls not allowed.

VIMALA. Says who?

GODSE. Says us. Right, Madhav?

Beat.

MADHAV. I'm not very good at cricket or wrestling.

GODSE. If we play together, we can become strong men, the strongest in Baramathi.

MADHAV. Okay then.

VIMALA. I wish you hadn't changed. I wish you were a girl again!

GODSE. Don't ever say that again! I will clobber you.

VIMALA. You know what? I think you've become a stupid boy.

MADHAV *and* VIMALA *run away.*

1.11

GODSE (*to us*). The biggest change came like dawn. One day, I woke up and I could no longer smell jasmine. I felt empty. Bereft. The goddess was gone.

BABA. This was bound to happen, Lakshmi. How can he reach the goddess when he is so bitter all the time.

GODSE (*to us, hurt*). I didn't expect it though. Now I'm just like everyone else. I felt jilted. Had the goddess found a new mind – a female mind – so soon after me?

AAI. What do we do now? We don't have enough wheat and dal to last us a month.

Silence.

BABA. Nathuram, *son*. I'm depending on you to get a job and start supporting this family soon. I need to know if I can count on my eldest son to finish school, go to college and get a good job to support his younger siblings. Can I, Nathuram?

GODSE. Yes, Baba.

BABA. Good. Next week, you're going to Pune, where you'll stay and study in a school for poor boys like you. It's the only school I can afford right now.

GODSE. You can't do that, Baba! All my friends are here.

BABA. You have only two friends, and even they –

GODSE (*snapping his fingers; to us*). You don't need that.

…and lights go down on BABA *and* AAI.

Speaking of friends…

1.12

GODSE *is now in jail. 1948. A radio plays.* GODSE *listens with obvious glee.*

RADIO. This is All India Radio. At least fifteen people have been killed and dozens injured in various mob attacks in and around Bombay Presidency, in the aftermath of Gandhiji's assassination. Prime Minister Nehru / has urged all citizens to remain calm –

GODSE (*to us*). You hear that? This is the fire I started. No one, not even Nehru or Patel, can stop it now – (*Laughs.*) The age of Gandhi is finally over! We're now in the age of –

APTE. Godse!

In another cell, a figure moves towards the bars. It is
NARAYAN APTE, *thirty-seven.*

Oho, Nathuram! Fancy bumping into you here!

GODSE. Apte! (*Pause. To us.*) Narayan Apte. My good friend –
no, best friend. (*To* APTE.) They got you. Damn you! How?
All you had to do was –

APTE. Stay hidden? For how long? We both know it was only
a matter of time. I was already a bundle of nerves, jumping
at every door slam – no, this is better. Look! We're almost
roommates now!

GODSE (*to us*). Together, we were –

APTE. The two-man army! We're back together and that's all
that matters!

GODSE. Shh.

KISHEN *and* DAULAT *have entered.*

DAULAT. Oy, friend of Pakistan! Do you require a special
invitation to exercise.

GODSE. Curse me but be correct about it! I'm never a friend of
Pakistan!

KISHEN *and* DAULAT *unlock the cells.*

KISHEN. Step out! No lip from either of you!

GODSE *and* APTE *step out.*

Walk to the yard. All heads forward! One behind another.

The two prisoners walk slowly, APTE *in front of* GODSE.

GODSE (*whispers*). Any news of –

APTE. The mobs, yes.

(*Whispers.*) Nathuram, your singular act was a call to arms.
Together, we'll erase Partition. An undivided India will be
realised, wait and see!

KISHEN. Silence!

APTE. The ripple we created cannot be stilled! It is only a matter of time!

GODSE (*loudly*). Akhand Bharat –

APTE (*loudly*). Amar Rahe –

GODSE (*loudly*). Long live –

APTE (*loudly*). Undivided India!

DAULAT. What did we say?

> DAULAT *hits* GODSE *and* APTE *until both fall to the ground.*

KISHEN (*to* GODSE). Murderer!

DAULAT. Traitor!

APTE. He is our saviour, you fool!

> GODSE *and* APTE *writhing on the ground.*

We must stop this non-violent civil disobedience thing. It's bad for our health!

> GODSE *and* APTE *laugh.*

ACT TWO

2.1

1928. Pune.

GODSE (*to us*). The two-man army. Polar opposites. Calm to my angry. Clownish to my serious. Flamboyant to my drab. Yin and yang. Simpatico with each other from our very first meeting.

At a newspaper vendor's. A younger GODSE *and* APTE.

APTE. / The latest please.

GODSE. The latest please.

GODSE *and* APTE *smile awkwardly.*

SELLER. Which one?

APTE. / All of them.

GODSE. All of them.

GODSE *and* APTE *laugh awkwardly. The* SELLER *brings them a bunch of newspapers.*

APTE. / You first.

GODSE. You first.

Both laugh.

APTE. / Apte.

GODSE. Godse.

Both laugh. The VENDOR *gives them the papers. Both read a newspaper.*

/ Bloody Gandhi.

APTE. Bloody Gandhi.

They look at each other in wonder.

I'll see you then.

GODSE. Don't be so sure!

APTE *laughs and makes to leave.* GODSE *is loath to let him go.*

(*To us, but still with* APTE *in that moment.*) I know I've put the cart before the horse and have gone too far ahead in time. We must go back a few years to 1920.

GODSE *watches him leave.*

GANDHI *enters.*

2.2

Spotlight on GANDHI, *now fifty-one, amidst a crowd. 1920.*

GANDHI. The Rowlatt Act must go.

GODSE (*to us*). The Rowlatt Act, a tyrannical leglislation meant to quell the rising tide of nationalism by any means necessary.

GANDHI. Do you know what the act does? It allows the police powers to arrest a person without a reason, charge or trial and keep them in jail indefinitely. It is designed to deny Indians of all real freedom. Are we going to keep quiet? No! Because to stay quiet in the face of evil is to be complicit in that very evil.

GODSE (*to us*). I call it the big betrayal. The response to Gandhi's call for peaceful protest against the Rowlatt Act was huge, especially in Punjab. Jallianwala Bagh. Does the name ring any bells? No Indian can ever forget. In the name of law and order a British general – Dyer – at a gathering at

a fairground on a sacred day, blocked all exits and without
a warning ordered his soldiers to fire. On ten thousand
innocent people. One thousand two hundred were killed,
though the British say only a few hundred.

GANDHI. * In South Africa, I discovered that as a man and as
an Indian, I had no rights. Or rather, I discovered that I had
no rights as a man because I was an Indian. I returned home
and I see more of the same. British law is not applied to us as
it is to the British.

GODSE (*to us*). A massacre to defend the Rowlatt Act.

GANDHI. We will not tolerate injustice. Boycott not just
British industries, but also their schools, their courts. All
those working for the government, in whatever way, step
down. Resign. * Stand with me as civil, but disobedient
brothers.

GODSE (*to us*). He called it the non-cooperation movement.
The goal, more than just the withdrawal of the act –

GANDHI. We demand swaraj. Self-rule.

GODSE (*to us*). All of India, people of all religions and all
walks of life became part of a mammoth resistance
movement on a scale never seen before. When he spoke,
everyone listened. When he said 'do', everyone did. Yes,
including me.

MITHUN, *forty, enters. He looks* GODSE *in the eye as he
walks past. For a moment,* MITHUN, GODSE *and*
GANDHI *are part of the same memory, before* GANDHI
leaves.

2.3

MITHUN *walks to his spot by the school gate.*

GODSE (*to us*). I was only twelve at my new school and things happened so fast.

MITHUN *pops a paan* (*betel leaf*) *into his mouth.*

(*To* MITHUN.) It was an error of judgement – you know that, right?

MITHUN *catches hold of* GODSE*'s shirt. Beat.*

MITHUN. Which class are you escaping from?

We are now in 1922. A school in Pune.

I asked you a question.

GODSE. English.

MITHUN. The other boys usually run away from history.

GODSE. Learning the language of our oppressors is like letting a foreign organism inhabit your bloodstream. If it stays there too long it changes the way you think and feel and move.

MITHUN *releases* GODSE.

MITHUN. The wall is lower near the playground.

GODSE (*to us*). Mithun, the school watchman. He let me play truant every now and then. He didn't say much, but when he did –

MITHUN. Oh, special one! Why is it that you never play with the other boys?

GODSE. They're boring and stupid.

MITHUN. I saw them taunt you at the canteen the other day.

GODSE. You saw wrong.

MITHUN. Come here, boy. Sit here.

No, like this. (*Demonstates.*) Like a man. Do you understand what I'm saying? In schools like this, you cannot be seen to be different. You must learn to walk and sit and do things, like them.

Another day.

Sit up straight. Look at me. Look at my shoulders. You boys, you may look at my moustache and laugh. But with shoulders like these do you feel like laughing? Watch and learn.

GODSE (*to us, squaring up his shoulders*). I learnt to sit like a man – (*Spreads his thighs*.) walk like one – (*Demonstrates*.) I took part in sports with confidence. Slowly but surely I was erasing all signs of Nathu and shaping myself into the Nathuram I wanted to be. I also discovered a few things about Mithun. One, he disappeared from his post by the school gate every now and then. And two, he had a second job unknown to school authorities.

MITHUN *sticks a poster on a wall*. GODSE *sneaks up behind him and picks up a poster.*

'British Bastards Go Home!' –

MITHUN. Give me that!

MITHUN *grabs* GODSE.

You've seen nothing. Not a word about this, understand? Do you understand?

GODSE. Yes.

Pause.

'Reward for killing the' – are people going to kill the Viceroy?

MITHUN. No.

GODSE. But it says –

MITHUN. You're a child. It's none of your business what adults do.

GODSE *moves away but doesn't leave.*

GODSE. Killing is not the solution.

MITHUN. I agree. I'm not killing though, am I? Listen, Godse,
I have six children. How do I feed them? On the peanuts
I get from guarding children like you? I have a bigger enemy
than the British and it's called hunger. Go away!

GODSE (*as he leaves*). I keep returning to the day that followed
and all the roads I didn't take.

2.4

A paan shop. Two PEOPLE, *the* PAANWALA, MITHUN *and
a British* POLICEMAN. *They all look at an upside-down poster
near the little mobile stall. The* POLICEMAN *holds a torn
poster of the Viceroy. Everyone is tense.* GODSE *enters quietly.*

POLICEMAN. I'll ask you once again slowly, who stuck the
poster up?

1 (*in Marathi*). Not me.

POLICEMAN. In English.

1. Not me, sahib. Working… fields full day.

2. Out of town, sahib. Home come only today morning.

PAANWALA. I make a paan, sahib? Fresh tobacco. It good.
You chew and chew and chew, spit become red then swallow.

GODSE *sidles up to* MITHUN.

MITHUN (*hisses under his breath*). What are you doing here?
Go back to school. This is not the place for you.

POLICEMAN. Do you know what I think? It's simply not
possible that none of you saw the man who did this. You get
to know what goes on in the next village without a telegram
or newspaper. Yet you don't know who stuck this right next
to this shop.

PAANWALA. The fellow does poster business when we sleep.

POLICEMAN. Do you all know what the Rowlatt Act is?

CROWD. Yes.

POLICEMAN. Good, now you know how powerful I am.

(*Re:* GODSE.) Who's this?

PAANWALA. He just follow, and follow, and follow our
Mithun... like a tail.

The crowd laughs.

POLICEMAN. Like a tail, aye? Then you must be the head.

MITHUN. Mithun, sahib.

POLICEMAN. Did you put up the poster, Mithun?

MITHUN. No, sahib.

POLICEMAN. Perhaps I should interrogate your appendage.

MITHUN. Sahib, he's a boy –

POLICEMAN. Where were you last night? (*Pause.*) Why are
you looking at him?

MITHUN. He very stupid. I ask him Marathi?

POLICEMAN. No! No one speaks in the vernacular here.
Understand?

GODSE *is about to flee but the* POLICEMAN *has got a firm
hold on him.*

Where were you last night?

GODSE *is in a quandary – to lie or tell the truth.*

Answer me, boy.

GODSE *spots a paan and quickly stuffs it in his mouth and
chews as if his life depended on it.*

Were you in your room in bed?

MITHUN. Yes – He say yes!

POLICEMAN. You're lying. Do you know what we do to lying
boys?

GODSE *does not respond*.

We put them in cells with no windows or food for weeks and – gently coax the truth out of them. With my stick. This stick here is best friends with truth. Who put the posters up?

GODSE *does not respond*.

(*To* GODSE.) In that case, it must be you.

GODSE *tries to flee but he's in the* POLICEMAN*'s iron grip*.

MITHUN. Sahib, please, he stupid boy –

POLICEMAN. Who has seen something.

MITHUN. Did you see who did it?

GODSE *shakes his head*.

He say no.

POLICEMAN. Spit it out and answer, lad.

PAANWALA. Swallow it, Godse.

POLICEMAN. What did you say?

PAANWALA. I ask swallow.

1. He can't.

2. Is it his first time with paan?

POLICEMAN. Speak bloody English, you louts! SPIT THE DAMN THING OUT NOW!

GODSE *spits. Red spittle splashes on* POLICEMAN*'s shirt. Beat.*

PAANWALA. I told you to swallow, you oaf!

POLICEMAN *hits* MITHUN *with the baton*.

GODSE. Stop!

POLICEMAN. So the tail has a mouth. Who put the posters up?

The POLICEMAN *hits* MITHUN *again*.

Oh look! I hit the head, the tail hurts. Sorry, people. I'm going to have to take the head in to the station.

MITHUN. No! I have family. I innocent.

POLICEMAN (*to* MITHUN). You spit on me, you spit on a man of the uniform. That's sedition.

GODSE (*to* PAANWALA). That was me. You saw that! I did that! Tell him in English!

Please... please... don't arrest. Arrest me.

PAANWALA. Godse, shh. He's sahib. We don't have a say in this.

GODSE (*to* MITHUN). I will get you out, Mithun Dada! I'll fight this for you! I promise you.

PAANWALA *muffles* GODSE's *mouth with his hand as the* POLICEMAN *takes* MITHUN *away.*

2.5

As GODSE *sets up a protest banner:*

GODSE (*to us*). I wasn't going to take this lying down. I was goddess touched! Saving Mithun was in my destiny. I had a plan of action. A hunger strike at school – in the exact template Gandhi had given the world. No food. Just water and a lot of noise.

GODSE *and* BOYS. Long live Gandhiji! Down with the British! Down with the Rowlatt Act! Release Mithun!

GODSE. Morning after a full breakfast.

SCHOOLBOYS *and* GODSE *with posters and banners chant slogans.*

GODSE *and* BOYS. Release Mithun! Down with the Rowlatt Act!

GODSE (*to us*). One hour later.

GODSE *and* BOYS (*less energetic*). Release Mithun! Down with the British!

BOY 1. Why isn't anyone coming to negotiate with us?

GODSE. Ahimsa is all about patience.

(*To us*.) Two hours later.

GODSE *and* BOYS. Release Mithun! Down with the Rowlatt Act!

The BOYS *are bored but one or two are energetic and chant, but sporadically.*

BOY 1. You said they'd be begging us to return to class.

GODSE. They want us to give up. We won't.

Down with the Rowlatt Act! Release Mithun!

(*To us*.) Three hours later.

The BOYS *lounge about with their banners.*

Long live Gandhiji! Vande Mataram!

(*To us*.) Lunchtime.

The bell rings.

BOY 1. The canteen is open.

GODSE. Remember our mission.

The BOYS *are desperately hungry. One by one all the* BOYS, *except* GODSE, *leave.*

Come back, you cowards!

Some time passes. GODSE *is all alone.*

(*To us*.) It's evening now. Darkness clouds my eyes, but my nose, it detects every single meal being cooked within half a mile. Potatoes, lentils, biryanis. By dinner –

The canteen bell rings.

I too… caved in.

GODSE *puts away his banner and leaves.*

(*To us.*) A week later, I came to know –

PAANWALA. Mithun is no more. The British have hanged him.

GODSE. What?

PAANWALA. I'm sorry, Godse.

GODSE *struggles not to break down.*

GODSE. Did they say why?

PAANWALA. They said he spat at a sahib.

GODSE. But he didn't. I did!

GODSE *is gutted.* PAANWALA *pats* GODSE*'s back in
commiseration.* GODSE *shrugs his hand off.*

PAANWALA. Who are we to question the law? He was a good
man.

GODSE. He was a shit watchman.

Lights out on PAANWALA.

2.6

GODSE (*to us*). I was Baramathi's spit champion. I could have
spat anywhere. No! It was not my fault! How was a child to
understand the power games of the Empire? Mithun's
murderers must have their comeuppance. There was only one
man in the entire country who could get Mithun justice. All
my hopes were vested now in this man and his non-
cooperation movement.

Lights on NEHRU, *thirty-three,* PATEL, *forty-seven,*
JINNAH, *forty-six, and* GANDHI, *fifty-two. It is 1922.*

NEHRU. The world is writing about us in awe, Bapu. *New York
Times, Washington Post* –

JINNAH. I think the British are close to capitulating –

PATEL. It's been a huge success, no doubt, except for one
    incident –

GANDHI. What incident?

Pause.

NEHRU. In a town called… (*Referring to a newspaper.*) Chauri
    Chaura –

JINNAH. Never heard of it –

PATEL (*to* JINNAH). It's somewhere in Central India –

GANDHI. What happened in Chauri Chaura?

NEHRU. People had been protesting – peacefully enough in the
    beginning, just as you wished, Bapu. And then things got out
    of hand. The police fired a few shots in the air, to get the
    crowd to settle, but one thing led to another –

JINNAH. To cut a long story short, the police fired at the
    crowd. The crowd went amok and chased the policemen into
    their station, locked up the door and set it on fire. Anyone
    who tried to escape was hacked to death.

GANDHI. How many dead?

NEHRU. Twenty-two policemen. Three civilians.

GANDHI. This is savagery.

NEHRU. It's a one-off incident, Bapu –

JINNAH. A sad, unfortunate incident, Mr Gandhi. We must
    strongly and immediately condemn the violence.

NEHRU. And request our people to maintain calm and order at
    all times –

PATEL. And add that for the sake of the nation, we must push
    on with our movement.

GANDHI. Violence begets violence.

Pause.

PATEL. Bapu?

GANDHI. I take full responsibility for the deaths. I will take a fast of atonement. (*Pause*.) And I am suspending the movement.

Beat.

GODSE (*to* GANDHI). What?

JINNAH. You can't be serious!

PATEL. No, no! Not at this stage, Bapu. We've started to make progress!

NEHRU. Are you going to penalise an entire country for the missteps of a few?

GANDHI. This is a tinderbox that will lead to genocide.

GODSE (*to* GANDHI). Genocide? Oh come on!

PATEL. I, I understand where you're coming from. We can use Chauri Chaura as a lesson. Teach people not to react to provocation. But please do not dismantle a successful campaign.

JINNAH. I have always been uncomfortable with your anarchic way of protest, Mr Gandhi. But our goal is very, very close.

NEHRU. We cannot lose our hard-earned momentum. Self-determination is reachable –

GANDHI. We are quick to take offence. We've been servants for far too long. We don't know how to be masters – of ourselves or of our own land.

PATEL. Please, for a moment, just consider. We've made the Empire sit up and take notice. If you call it off now, it will be seen as a victory for them –

GANDHI. We cannot build a country if we ignore the poor. Living in forgotten towns like Chauri Chaura.

GODSE (*to* GANDHI). You're not stopping now!

GANDHI. I've decided. I'm leaving the front-line politics to work at the grassroots, in the villages. Rural India is where our future lies.

NEHRU. We need you here!

PATEL. Don't do this, Bapu. It's suicidal.

GODSE. Jinnah, tell him no!

JINNAH. Well, it appears that you have decided for all of us.

GODSE (*to* NEHRU, PATEL *and* JINNAH). Are you going to let him? What sort of leaders are you? (*To* GANDHI.) Mithun's death can't be for nothing! He was innocent, he deserved justice!

MITHUN *emerges from the darkness.*

MITHUN. Why didn't you listen to me?

Did you think I was beneath you?

GODSE (*to* GANDHI). I trusted you to fight for him. Look at you, running away at the first sign of blood, like a coward! You hide behind your ahimsa, you give everyone false hope. You pretend to fight for us, but you abandon us when we need you!

MITHUN. Did you think you were special?

GODSE (*to* GANDHI). Are we so unimportant that our deaths don't matter? You are not the man I thought you were! Our great land does not deserve you! You Gandhi – ji. You no longer deserve ji. You selfish, egoistic narcissist! I spit on you!

For a moment, MITHUN, GANDHI *and* GODSE *are part of the same memory.* BABA *enters.*

2.7

BABA. Congratulations, Nathuram! You're a murderer now.

GODSE. What?

Lights down on MITHUN *and* GANDHI. *It is 1928. The* GODSE *house.* AAI, BABA *and* GODSE. BABA *has* GODSE*'s report card in his hand.*

BABA. Congratulations, Nathuram! You're a matric fail now. How will you find a good job? You have to retake your English exam.

GODSE. I'll still fail.

BABA. Because of just one exam, you won't have a damn career, and we won't have a damn future because you, you were too busy getting into trouble –

GODSE . You don't understand.

BABA. Damn right I don't. You'd better start earning your keep. You are eighteen, a man now, and I cannot subsidise you any more.

GODSE. No, but you were happy to be subsidised by me before, weren't you?

AAI. Let's just be grateful he's not obsessing about Gandhi any more, alright? Let's all just calm down and eat.

BABA. I won't let you become a loafer or a thug. So listen up, young man. You'll learn a trade starting immediately and then you'll ply that trade when we move to Ratnagiri.

GODSE. Ratnagiri?

AAI. Yes, Baba got his posting orders just today.

GODSE. Do I get to choose my trade or are you going to decide, again, who I should be?

AAI. Of course you can choose.

GODSE. I'd like to be a tailor. (*To us*.) I don't know why I said that.

BABA (*to* AAI). I'd have chosen a manly trade for him.

AAI. Shh. Tailor is a splendid idea! (*To* BABA.) It's a manlier profession than delivering post if you ask me. And now I can get my blouses stitched for free!

2.8

GODSE (*to us*). Ratnagiri, in West India. A sleepy, pointless little nowhere town. It's no Bombay or Pune, where a young man like me could flourish. (*Re: the townsfolk.*) No, they're not bustling about. They're all busy going nowhere. Like me. It is 1928 now.

1928. Ratnagiri. A small tailor's shop on a busy street. GODSE holds out a shirt to KISHORE, fifty-five, who studies it. KISHORE measures it meticulously. GODSE waits in silence.

(*To us.*) Of all the professions I could have chosen!

KISHORE. How many times do I have to tell you, we need to make allowance for shrinkage?

GODSE. Kishore, master tailor of Ratnagiri.

I have given a quarter-inch –

KISHORE. Aiyyayyy! That's the allowance for Gandhi's handspun not Manchester cotton. Redo the whole thing with my measurements. (*Getting back to marking fabrics with chalk.*) My life was simpler before Gandhi, when fabrics were standardised.

GODSE (*to us*). I confess I was disappointed. Was this to be my life's purpose, to squeeze my waking hours through eyes of endless needles, to hem and picot till I grow old? Then, he...

VINAYAK SAVARKAR, *forty-five, enters the shop.*

...walked in. Ramrod straight as if he'd bend for no earthly force.

GODSE *sits straight.*

GODSE. Kaka! We have a customer.

KISHORE. Ohhh, Savarkarji! What an honour! (*To GODSE.*) Don't you know who that is? Aiyyayy! Which stone were you hiding under? He is Savarkar, the revolutionary! The man who jumped into the sea off the coast of France and swam all night to Marseilles to evade the British –

SAVARKAR. Only to get caught on the shore. Pranam, Kishore.

KISHORE. Only because one of our own betrayed you. Oh how
   my blood boils at the thought of all the years spent in the
   harshest prison of the Empire! (*To* GODSE.) Why are you
   standing there gawking? Get a chair!

GODSE (*to us, as he fetches the chair*). Savarkar had eyes like
   a hawk and smelt of sandalwood.

KISHORE. Sorry about that – new assistant.

GODSE (*to us*). He'd survived thirteen years in jail. And then
   was sent to this nowhere town, Ratnagiri, where he wasn't
   allowed to participate in political activity of any kind, or
   leave the area, basically house arrest.

SAVARKAR. Make me a new coat, Kishore.

   SAVARKAR *studies* GODSE. GODSE *is unnerved.*

GODSE. Is this foreign wool?

KISHORE. Obviously homespun. Look at the count –

SAVARKAR. Are you one of his acolytes?

GODSE. Do you mean Gandhi? Do you know him?

KISHORE. Pffft! Know Gandhi! He came here to visit him the
   moment he heard Savarkarji was here.

   While KISHORE *measures and* GODSE *jots down the
   measurements in his notebook,* SAVARKAR *talks:*

SAVARKAR. Well, he tried to talk me into embracing ahimsa.
   He thought my incarceration would have changed me!
   (*Laughs.*) I first met Gandhiji when I was a law student in
   London –

KISHORE. Note down –

SAVARKAR. I was twenty-six, and heart-deep in our bloody,
   messy freedom struggle.

KISHORE. Forty-three –

SAVARKAR. I was already organising a band of revolutionaries across Europe to take on the bloody British –

KISHORE. Breathe in –

SAVARKAR. I was learning weaponry and bomb-making to ready my team for a war –

KISHORE. Forty and thirty-seven-point-four –

SAVARKAR. – while your Gandhiji was nearly forty years old and living a comfortable life in South Africa –

KISHORE. Seventeen –

SAVARKAR. – and reluctant to return to India. After all the years in Cellular Jail, I come out and what do I find?

KISHORE. Fifteen. Raise your arms –

SAVARKAR. That man is not only at the forefront of Indian politics but was also being called a great soul for spouting his non-violence nonsense. A bloody mahatma.

KISHORE. Twenty-six and a half. Drop your arms –

SAVARKAR. It's an absolute travesty of all the real sacrifices people like me have made.

KISHORE. Seven –

SAVARKAR. Go on, wear one of those Gandhi handspuns and go on hunger strikes. A surefire way to get independence. By not doing a thing! (*Laughs.*) Thank you, Kishore. Let me know when the coat is ready!

GODSE. Wait! I'm not his follower. I don't believe the Gandhi way will lead us to freedom.

SAVARKAR. So are you going to sit here and sew buttons or are you going to do something about it?

SAVARKAR *leaves*.

GODSE (*to us*). The antithesis of Gandhi is in this town! Ah, the utter deliciousness of when random events and choices come together. So all you sceptics and rationalists here, may I please use the F-word here? Fate.

2.9

GODSE (*to us*). I smelt him before I saw him.

SAVARKAR *walks up to the shop*.

SAVARKAR. Is my coat ready?

GODSE. Yes. Would you like to try it on?

SAVARKAR *tries on the coat in front of a mirror.* GODSE *tries to speak to him several times, but chickens out.*

SAVARKAR. It fits well.

GODSE. A lot of hard work went into it.

Pause.

SAVARKAR. If you have something to say, say it.

GODSE. If there's an odd job that you want done, I could do it for you.

SAVARKAR (*hands over money*). I don't. Give this to Kishore.

SAVARKAR *is on his way out*.

GODSE. I... I am a good learner. I can do anything you want me to.

SAVARKAR. Which means you don't have any usable skill. You should stick to your buttons.

GODSE *is disappointed*.

GODSE (*to us*). Look, I'm not discouraged. One can't hope to be a daredevil's follower if one gives up at the first 'no'. Right? Another day –

SAVARKAR. No.

GODSE. Another day –

SAVAKAR. No.

GODSE. Another day. (*Pause.*) I... It's a lovely day, isn't it?

SAVARKAR (*snaps*). Boy! – Let me make this clear. I don't intend to return to that hellhole prison because some pimply teenager suddenly got it in his head that he wants to play freedom fighter.

GODSE *is disappointed*.

GODSE (*to us*). Sometimes, it's not enough if the time and place are right. Sometimes you also need the right ally. Another day.

GODSE *waits*. APTE *enters*.

APTE. You!

GODSE. / You!

They laugh.

APTE. Godse, right?

GODSE. Yes.

APTE. Do you remember my name?

GODSE. Sorry, no. I am not good with names… Apte.

APTE *laughs*.

APTE. Are you also –

GODSE. Waiting for him? Yes. I've not been successful.

APTE. Never fear, Apte is here.

SAVARKAR *walks in. He takes a look at them. Beat*.

Oh he's going to turn back. Quick come with me!

SAVARKAR *turns back but is confronted by* APTE *and* GODSE.

Vande Mataram! I'm Apte from Pune –

SAVARKAR. A wasted trip I'm afraid –

APTE (*speaking fast*). I'm a student of Bombay University, member of several patriotic student organisations –

SAVARKAR (*uninterested*). Am I to congratulate you?

APTE. President of the university debate team, member of the long-distance swimming team. You've inspired me –

SAVARKAR. You're too kind –

APTE. I seek your guidance on how I – we – could contribute to the nationalist –

SAVARKAR. I'm in a rush, sorry –

GODSE *grabs* SAVARKAR's *collar aggressively and stops him.*

APTE. Godse!

SAVARKAR *is stunned, but is now interested.*

GODSE. You can spare us two minutes! We are brothers. Your people, our people, we go back a long way.

Pause.

SAVARKAR. Two minutes only.

GODSE. The youth are rudderless, Gandhi is god-knows-where, doing hermit things – There is a huge leadership void. We cannot think of anyone braver or more cunning –

APTE. What he said.

GODSE. We need those qualities to win against the British –

APTE. Be our leader, we'll gather foot soldiers, we'll start our countermovement. There are many like us, full-blooded youth, willing to do anything for our Motherland.

SAVARKAR. Are you really?

GODSE. / Yes.

APTE. Yes.

SAVAKAR. Are you ready to die?

APTE. In a heartbeat.

GODSE. What he said.

(To us.) He heard us out that day. While he didn't say so in so many words, he became our mentor. Hope smells a lot like sandalwood.

2.10

1929. SAVARKAR, APTE *and* GODSE.

SAVARKAR. Have you ever wondered how a small island with a tenth of our population could conquer and colonise us? (*Pause.*) Think… or has British education completely enslaved your minds?

GODSE. They had money –

APTE. And military strength –

SAVARKAR. Oh, bright sparks, we were one of the wealthiest regions in the world. We had more than enough people to form several armies! Yet the white men who came to trade with us became our rulers. How, Godse? Apte?

GODSE *and* APTE *think.* SAVARKAR *is annoyed.*

Oh for… Because we bloody let them! Because they saw our humanity as weakness to be exploited! We are docile and peace-loving, too bloody welcoming of other cultures. 'You want to invade us, oh welcome!' Yet, how many settlers on our land have tried to assimilate with us, us the dominant, indigenous culture of the region?

GODSE. Not the British.

SAVARKAR. Well, not the Muslims either.

GODSE. Muslims?

SAVARKAR (*snaps*). Yes, Godse, Muslims! Who invaded us from Persia and stayed on and ruled over us before the British. They live today on our land as if they're not Indians but Persians. That, Godse, Apte, if you can divert some energy into thinking, is the crux of the problem. Their loyalty does not lie with their Motherland, which is India, but with their holy land in another part of the world. How can you expect lasting peace between Hindus and Muslims with such an attitude? How can you expect any concession from the British when there are enemies within us?

GANDHI *emerges from the darkness.* APTE *moves into the darkness.*

The Germans have it right. The only key to nation building is homogeneity. One culture, one nation. Minority cultures must embrace the practices of the majority culture. I am an atheist but I'm a Hindu too. Hindu-ness is a way of life, our way of life, and it must become everyone's. Our goal shouldn't just be an independent India but an independent Hindu India.

GODSE (*to us*). That was the first time I heard of a Hindu nation.

For a moment all three are on stage. Lights out on SAVARKAR. GANDHI *and* GODSE *face each other, each seemingly in the other's path.*

GANDHI. Are you lost?

GODSE. What?

GANDHI. Don't you smell it, the jasmine?

GODSE. What are you doing? Go away!

GANDHI. I expect much more of you.

GODSE. Enough! This is my story and I'll tell it my way. Why don't you just stay dead?

GANDHI *disappears. Darkness.*

Interval.

ACT THREE

3.1.

GODSE (*to us*). Welcome back! So, you've voluntarily returned to the company of a murderer. Think about that as you settle down. Look around you. If violence enters this room, what will you all do? All I'm saying is, given the right circumstances, even you could turn into... well, me. A man faced with a tough choice, forced to do the unthinkable. For the sake of something bigger than him.

DAULAT *and* KISHEN *enter.*

KISHEN. Godse! Apte! Step forward, criminals!

GODSE *steps forward towards the cell bars.* APTE *too.*

Mr Nathuram Godse and Mr Narayan Apte, I hereby inform you both that the date of your trial has been fixed and will begin next week. Any questions, you may further take up with concerned authorities.

APTE. Who would that be?

DAULAT. I am not the authority nor am I concerned.

DAULAT *and* KISHEN *titter.*

KISHEN. Any news from Mumbai, Daulat bhai? A couple of our prisoners here keep expecting something big to happen –

DAULAT. Big?

KISHEN. Nation-wide big, bhai. Like Gandhiji's independence movement.

DAULAT. Oho! Our prisoners think they're better than our Bapuji, is it?

KISHEN *and* DAULAT *titter.*

Actually, it's deathly quiet everywhere, bhai. It's like everyone is waiting for the trial to begin and all co-conspirators sent to the gallows.

GODSE. All co-conspirators? There was no one else.

KISHEN. Were you so stupid you didn't realise you were bringing others down with you?

DAULAT. Anyone who has assisted you in the assassination will be brought to trial. For example, your mentor Savarkar has been arrested.

Pause.

Oh you didn't really think this through, did you?

DAULAT *and* KISHEN *laugh.*

GODSE. Enough of these two idiots! Let's go on to something more interesting.

The prison cells and the POLICEMEN *disappear.*

3.2

SAVARKAR. Gandhi's secularism is biased. He is quick to condemn a Hindu murderer of a Muslim but is awash with sympathy for a Muslim murderer of a Hindu. Our Muslim compatriots now wrongly think they are indispensable to our struggle. * It is about time we look at them in the eye and tell them, we will fight this war against the British, with you, without you, in spite of you. And we will win this war.

GODSE. The key word here is fight.

SAVARKAR. Yes. Ahimsa is a false god. Pacifism in the face of violence is stupidity. Why would you knowingly martyr yourself when nothing useful can be achieved from your death?

APTE. Are you saying we needn't sacrifice our lives for our struggle?

SAVARKAR. On the contrary. But death is not the opening gambit. It is the endgame. Your queen's sacrifice must take down his king, not his pawn. Death must be worth it.

GODSE *is starstruck with the idea.*

APTE. A good death...

GODSE. A perfect death.

3.3

At the tailor shop. A MUSLIM CUSTOMER *enters with an armful of fabrics.* KISHORE *and* GODSE *are their desks, working.*

MUSLIM CUSTOMER. As-salaam-alaikkum.

KISHORE. Walaikkum-asalaam.

MUSLIM CUSTOMER. Two shirts for me. Please can you have them ready before Ramzan?

KISHORE. Yes, of course. Take his measurements, Godse.

GODSE *gets the notebook.*

GODSE. Jai Shri Ram!

MUSLIM CUSTOMER. Yes, I'd like two pockets and a collar that –

GODSE (*with aggression*). Jai Shri Ram!

KISHORE. Godse! Enough! Oh please, forgive him! He's gone mad. I'll take your measurements –

GODSE. Jai Shri Ram! Come on say it –

KISHORE. Godse! Just stop it!

MUSLIM CUSTOMER. Kishore, this is preposterous. Are all customers required to prove their patriotism here or is it just Muslims?

GODSE. It's just three goddamn words –

KISHORE. Godse, just shut up and do your job. (*To* MUSLIM CUSTOMER.) I am so sorry. Please, please sit down, may I get you some tea, let me –

MUSLIM CUSTOMER. I think I'll find someone else, thank you very much.

MUSLIM CUSTOMER *walks off in a huff.*

KISHORE. May I just remind you that this is my shop, and you're just an apprentice. My rules, understand? You'll treat all my customers with respect –

GODSE. It shouldn't be a difficult thing to say. Unless you're a traitor.

Lights back on SAVARKAR *and lights down on* KISHORE.

SAVARKAR. Find your enemy. Lock your target. Find all that is different between you and him. Feed those differences. Nurture your rage. The moment you find commonalities with your foe, you become weak. If you are to win this battle, if you are to win any battle, it is by widening the gap between yourself and him.

GODSE (*to us*). If beliefs were bricks, he was building me a fortress on the rubble of the house I'd been living in. For the first time, I felt I could be someone truly important.

SAVARKAR. Apte, will you get me the latest foreign newspapers?

Here's a list of books for you. Pune has good libraries.

GODSE. I'll go right away and check them out.

SAVARKAR (*hands him money*). Oh while you're there, can you get me some black ink for my pen?

GODSE. Of course.

As for Gandhi, I hadn't thought about him in months.

VIMALA (*off*). Liar!

> VIMALA *emerges from the darkness with a plate of food and a salt shaker.*

> Gandhiji wasn't idling away was he, nose ring?

> VIMALA *shakes salt on to her food.*

GODSE. Go away! You have no place in my story.

VIMALA. And yet here I am!

GODSE (*to us*). Sorry about this. Look – She's of no importance, narratively speaking. And no, I'm not lying.

VIMALA (*to* GODSE). Gandhiji had been unifying our people, educating them. And now he returned.

GODSE (*to us*). After eight long years. And our people became stupid gullible fools again –

VIMALA. No, excited, hopeful again –

GODSE (*to us*). He was a sham master! A shameless sham master gambling with our future! What new calamity was he going to unleash now?

VIMALA (*to* GODSE). What he was about to unleash was… a revolution.

3.4

1930. Lights on in GANDHI's *Sabarmati Ashram.* NEHRU, *forty-one, and* PATEL, *fifty-five, are seated on cushions on the floor.* GANDHI, *sixty-one, and* VIMALA, *twenty, are making rotis.*

VIMALA (*to us*). Gandhi's Sabarmati Ashram. 1930.

GODSE (*to us*). Ah. So that's where we are. Our 'leaders' are scheming to relaunch Gandhi in mainstream politics –

VIMALA (*to* GODSE). What they're planning is a protest unlike any other. Against Britain's repressive salt taxes. A march from the ashram to the salt pans of the western coast. This would inaugurate Bapu's civil disobedience movement.

(*To* NEHRU *and* PATEL.) Lunch is served. Please join us.

NEHRU. Oh we couldn't impose –

GANDHI. Nonsense. We've been expecting you. What news do you have?

NEHRU. Not very promising, I'm afraid. Only some of our friends have assured us that they'd join us.

GANDHI. How many?

NEHRU. Eighty.

GODSE (*to us, gleefully*). Not enough. Not barely enough!

NEHRU. And we don't know, of these eighty, how many would actually turn up.

PATEL. Bapu, if this fails, it is bound to be seen as a victory for the British and a major failure for you, for us.

NEHRU. Now that will be a disaster from which our movement – no, our country – cannot recover. No, I think we should postpone this. You need to re-establish your presence first.

GANDHI. No, my inner voice tells me the time is now. I hope you're hungry.

VIMALA *and* GANDHI *serve rotis and dal.*

VIMALA. He made the rotis and the dal himself.

GANDHI. Oh don't worry. I'm an excellent cook, am I not?

VIMALA. For an ascetic, yes, Bapu.

NEHRU. Thank you.

PATEL. Bapu, I'll be honest here, it's just salt. Protesting against the Empire's salt tax, it cannot capture public imagination. It is too inconsequential a thing.

VIMALA. We've been making and trading salt long before the British stepped foot on our soil.

GANDHI. She's right.

VIMALA. It's not inconsequential when they have complete monopoly over the manufacture and have imposed grossly unfair taxes –

PATEL. As they have with other products. Tea, / for instance.

NEHRU. Thank goodness, it's not a tea march. I could never climb a mountain to make a symbolic gesture of independence.

PATEL. It's already been done, in Boston.

GANDHI. We have sea on three sides. There's salt water in plenty. And the poor too like to eat, Patel bhai.

PATEL. Bapu. Our march may not have an actual impact with the British. We have to be ready for that.

GANDHI *gives them both plates of rotis.*

GANDHI. The march is not just symbolic. It is not just a deliberate violation of government rules. The march is meant to unite all our brothers and sisters, especially Hindus and Muslims, towards a common goal. Now, go on, eat.

PATEL *and* NEHRU *dip pieces of roti in dal and take a bite.*

NEHRU. Bapu. It's…

PATEL. Saltless.

GANDHI. Yes. Next to air and water, salt is the greatest necessity of life. It is sinful to tax it. People will come, rich and poor, because it's salt. Our cause is just, our means are strong and God is with us. Don't waste food.

PATEL *and* NEHRU *are still struggling with the rotis.*

PATEL. May I have some salt please?

3.5

GANDHI *walks to the sea.*

GODSE. This Dandi Salt March was an unmitigated disaster –

VIMALA *enters.*

VIMALA. You lying piece of shit! It was an extraordinary success, like nothing anyone had seen before –

GODSE. Why are you still here? When you're only a minor character in my life?

VIMALA. You tell me, nose ring. It's your head.

GODSE *snaps his fingers.* VIMALA *remains.*

GODSE. Go away, goddamit!

VIMALA *remains. They look at each other. Silence. She is not going away. Then resigned,* GODSE *continues:*

(*To us.*) The trek from Gandhi's Sabarmati Ashram to Dandi on the coast of the Arabian sea was a three-week journey – (*To* VIMALA.) What I tell them is my business. Leave me alone! (*To us.*) Look, she's wrong. I know what history books tell you and they're all wrong, false, made up, / one-sided –

VIMALA. Imagine a bald, bespectacled, sixty-year-old man in a dhoti and a shawl, walking briskly with the aid of just a stick. Eighty followers and friends walk beside or behind him. More join him at every crossroad, thousands more, at every pit stop. Rich, poor, farmer, teacher, educated, illiterate, all converging around a single figure: Gandhi. By the time the group reaches the salt-laden shores of Dandi, it's grown to sixty thousand. The speed at which our small group became a serpentine – and orderly – column of protesters was something to behold. Sixty thousand walking as one, nose ring.

GODSE. Fools!

GANDHI *finally reaches the sea.*

VIMALA. Imagine the smell of the sea, the feel of the wind on your face, the sound of the waves. Imagine too the excitement in the air, a palpable sense of defiance. And the pin-drop silence from those who've gathered as everyone waits for a cue from Gandhi. He steps forward, bends down…

GANDHI *bends down and scoops a handful of salt.*

…Takes a fist full of salt from the ground and holds it up high over his head. He opens his fist and displays it to everyone. Imagine the crystals of salt, sparkling in the morning sun.

GANDHI. This land is ours, this sea ours. Making salt is our birthright. * With this fistful of salt, we will shake the foundations of the British Empire. And we will not rest until we get Purna Swaraj. Complete independence. Freedom for India! Vande –

ALL. Mataram!

GANDHI. Bharat Mata Ki –

ALL. Jai!

GANDHI *lets the salt flow through his fingers into the ground.*

VIMALA. Imagine now the deafening roar of joy from the people as they too bend down for a handful of precious white grains. (*Pause.*) This, nose ring, is what you missed when you crossed over to the other side, the electrifying force of that moment. With just one fistful of salt, Bapu had placed the British Empire on notice.

3.6

GODSE. Enough! Shall I tell you what happened next? Shall I tell them? The next salt march. As expected by anyone with half a brain, Gandhi, his wife Kasturba and other leaders, were arrested before they set out. The marchers continued to the sea regardless. But this time, the British police were ready with their batons at the beach. (*To* VIMALA.) Shall I go on? (*To us*.) The marchers proceeded and the police struck them. Here's the thing: no marcher even raised an arm to defend himself. They all crumbled to the ground because the old man had said:

GANDHI. * Let the fist holding the salt be broken but there will be no voluntary surrender of the salt.

GODSE. Imagine now the sound of skull against thick wood. Then imagine hearing it over and over and over, three hundred times. The pristine shore is now littered with broken, moaning bodies. Imagine now the white, white grains of salt now stained a wretched red. All for a fistful of salt. For a bloody symbol. (*To* VIMALA.) They were just sixty. We were hundreds. Maths was on our side. He made us give up without a fight –

VIMALA. Protest is fight. Making salt is fight. Ahimsa is fight. Not resisting is fight. Our fight is principled fight.

GODSE. He's weakening us –

VIMALA. He's empowering us, the common people, the teeming millions. We don't need to be warriors. We don't need to be young or strong or know how to wield weapons. All we need is courage to face violence with love. The entire nation is coming together like never before. The whole world is watching us, watching the British government lose moral authority to govern us with every strike of the baton. Yes, nose ring, maths is on Bapu's side.

A judge's gavel sounds. Lights down on VIMALA.

3.7

The gavel sounds again. And we are in 1948. GODSE *and* APTE *stand in the defendants' cage.*

GODSE (*to us*). 1948. The Court of the Special Judge, Red Fort, Delhi, is now in session. I am Accused Number One, Apte Accused Number Two. Partners in crime, partners in resistance, partners in court.

APTE. I plead not guilty to all charges, your honour.

GODSE. I plead guilty to the charge of murder. I planned alone. I acted alone. The decision to kill Gandhi was mine and mine alone. My act of violence should be punished with another act of violence and ahimsa should be eradicated with my death.

AAI *has entered.*

AAI. Nathuram!

Nathuram!

3.8

We crash into 1936 at the tailor shop. AAI *has entered the shop.* KISHORE *and* GODSE *are at their work tables.*

KISHORE. Your mother is here. (*To* AAI.) Please keep it quick. He's got a load of work to do.

AAI. I'm here to get a blouse stitched. (*To* KISHORE.) Not you, him. (*To* GODSE.) I want it in a new design.

GODSE. You've only ever worn in one pattern.

AAI. It's time for a change. I want to go through a pattern book. Do you have one?

Beat. KISHORE *passes* GODSE *a booklet, which he then hands over to* AAI. AAI *peruses the book.* GODSE *continues to stitch.* AAI *observes him.*

You didn't come home last night.

Where were you?

GODSE. In Pune.

AAI turns a page.

AAI. You leave before the dawn breaks. What do you do? Where do you go?

GODSE (*to* AAI). I don't have time for unimportant things.

AAI. We are not unimportant. We are family! You don't suddenly stop interacting with us.

GODSE. Aai.

KISHORE. Maybe you should do this at home –

AAI glares at KISHORE, *who goes back to work.*

AAI. I don't like you spending time with those friends of yours. Especially that fellow Apte.

KISHORE. Aiyyayy. I knew instantly he was the wrong sort. I see him with a new woman every time I go to Pune. Never with his wife.

AAI glares at him.

Sorry. I'll just go to another corner of my own shop so that my never-in assistant can have his privacy.

AAI. They're turning your head.

GODSE. They're more my family than...

AAI is hurt.

AAI. Nathu! You've started to see me as your enemy. Oh give me back the cloth! Don't bother stitching it. I'll go elsewhere –

GODSE. Aai –

AAI *leaves with her blouse fabric*.

KISHORE. Have we lost another customer?

GODSE (*to us*). I did not have time for sentiments, except those that serve the pursuit of my goal.

APTE *enters. For a moment,* KISHORE, *the shop,* APTE *and* GODSE *are in the same memory, before lights go down on* KISHORE *and the shop*.

Apte was both my best example and sole exception.

3.9

APTE. What the hell are we doing, Godse?

GODSE. What do you mean?

APTE. At our age, Savarkar had organised an armed rebellion. We should be spearheading the freedom struggle. We should be starting political parties. I thought he'd turn us into warriors. Instead we've become his fucking errand boys.

GODSE. Apte! Are you drunk?

APTE. Open your eyes, Godse. You're not going to be a Nehru to his Gandhi. You're not going to be his favourite.

GODSE. Not a word more –

APTE. You know why? Because you're too deferential to him, too damn servile –

GODSE *turns away*.

Go on, run away! Look at how you've castrated yourself to fit into his world –

GODSE *hits him. Beat.* GODSE *and* APTE *fight. It is messy
and violent. When they've vented their frustration, they lie
on the ground side by side. Then* APTE *laughs.*

This is the first active gesture you've made in a long time!

GODSE. You are drunk.

APTE. Never been more sober. Godse, we have betrayed our
bloodline! Our forefathers used to be the power behind the
Maratha throne! They fought with the Mughals and the East
India Company. And fucking won. We are not meant to be
like other caste Hindus! We are warriors! Do you know what
my friends are doing right now? They're organising and
training themselves. Forming militias. They'll be be ready to
fight the moment the Motherland calls for them. It's time for
action, Godse. We must take charge of our lives. Seize our
power! Win back our Hindu pride!

GODSE. Yes! Consolidate all Hindus!

APTE. Yes!

GODSE. Take on those who are diluting our Hindu-ness!

APTE. Yes!

GODSE. Those who kowtow to our colonisers –

APTE. Yes!

Pause.

/ Gandhi.

GODSE. Gandhi.

GODSE *and* APTE *look at each other and laugh.* APTE *and*
GODSE *are in the moment when – lights up on* VIMALA.

3.10

The gates of a Gandhi rally. We are in 1935. GODSE *is twenty-five and* APTE *twenty-four.* VIMALA *pursues them.*

GODSE (*to us*). So here we are in Pune. Gandhi is to be a keynote speaker here. In a sea of sycophants, we were going to be two rational, contrarian and loud voices.

VIMALA. Nathuram Godse! I knew I'd one day bump into you at some Gandhi rally or the other!

GODSE (*to us*). She just keeps showing up in my narrative like an unnecessary apostrophe.

VIMALA *reaches them.*

Remember I haven't seen her since I left home as a child.

GODSE*'s mannerisms become somewhat feminine through the rest of the segment.*

VIMALA. It's me, Vimala. The Warrior. (*To* APTE.) We were the Brilliant Bandits of Baramathi. He was our Spit Champion!

APTE (*to* GODSE). Godse! You never told me you had friends. (*To* VIMALA.) I'm Apte. (*To* GODSE.) Spit Champion?

VIMALA (*laughs*). Show him, Nathuram. His spit missiles had the most amazing trajectories. (*To* GODSE.) Or have you forgotten how to?

APTE. Godse, show me, show me!

GODSE (*hisses*). Stop thinking with your balls – remember our purpose!

APTE. Yes, let's both do that.

VIMALA. Come on, Nathuram Godse, show the world what powerful spitters folk from Baramathi are! Let's have a match. Shall I go first?

GODSE (*to* VIMALA). We aren't children any more. Have some shame.

Beat.

VIMALA. Oh, Bapu will be speaking at the rally in a short while. The child I knew wouldn't miss it for the world! You should go in now.

APTE. Shall we?

GODSE (*to* VIMALA). Are you an ashramite now?

VIMALA. Obviously. The question is: why aren't you?

APTE (*laughs*). Him? Why would –

GODSE. You disgust me – you… Muslim sympathiser!

VIMALA. What?

GODSE. Isn't this where traitors – sorry, 'secularists' – gather? Are we at the wrong meeting, Apte?

Pause.

VIMALA. Are you a Savarkarite now?

GODSE. A proud Savarkarite. And a patriot, unlike your bapu, who is intent on making our country effeminate.

VIMALA. Effeminate, Nathuram? You use that word? You of all people. Does your mentor know how you began? (*Re:* APTE.) Does he know?

APTE. What do you mean?

GODSE. We heard your leader reads from the Quran, the Bible and the Gita at his prayer meetings! You are offending all Hindus.

APTE. You are betraying our religion –

VIMALA. Inclusiveness is in our religion! We are not so different, Hindus, Muslims, Christians or Sikhs – please just listen – What do all religions have in common?

APTE. Gandhi?

GODSE *and* APTE *titter.*

GODSE. He's fucking everywhere!

VIMALA. Pursuit of truth, ahimsa.

APTE. He's relegating Hindus to the periphery of political power.

GODSE. He's diluting our culture –

VIMALA. Look at the crowd here. Every single person here, except you two, is ready to face the British with courage. What the hell are you two doing?

GODSE. What are we doing, Apte?

APTE. Protesting. Mohandas Gandhi –

GODSE. Hai hai!

APTE. Mohandas Gandhi –

GODSE. Hai / hai!

VIMALA. Have you been to jail? I have. Have you faced British baton? I have. What battles have you fought?

GODSE. That is enough!

VIMALA. Oh right, I forget, you're so messed up that even the goddess couldn't stand to be inside your brain.

Beat. GODSE *moves aggressively towards* VIMALA.

APTE. Godse.

VIMALA *stands her ground*.

VIMALA. Look, I have to go now. Are you going to join us?

Pause.

Come to our ashram. Spend some time with us. Let us try to understand each other. Bapu would love to talk to people like you.

GODSE. I can see it's a damn waste of time coming here. Let's go. Goodbye, Vimala.

VIMALA. The Nathuram of Baramathi would be so disappointed in you.

VIMALA *leaves*.

3.11

A few days later. The tailor shop. SAVARKAR, APTE *and*
GODSE. KISHORE *is at his usual spot.*

SAVARKAR. Let me get this straight. You travelled a hundred
    kilometres and left without saying a word to him.

APTE. Gandhi arrived late, didn't he? And we had the last bus
    to catch.

SAVARKAR. I've been wasting my time all these years.
    Cowards! My path is not the right one for you.

GODSE. No, no, it absolutely is the right –

SAVARKAR. Enough of words. Prove it. What are you willing
    to do for your Motherland? Are you willing to die?

GODSE. Yes.

SAVARKAR. Are you willing to kill?

    Pause.

    Thought so. You can't even say the words.

GODSE. They are just words! I have done everything you
    asked me to!

SAVARKAR. Have you done anything that I haven't asked you
    to? Godse? Do you have an ounce of initiative to do things
    on your own? You were the one who said you were going to
    a Gandhi rally to protest. Did you do it? No.

APTE. It's not his fault that Gandhi was late –

SAVARKAR. Was he? My sources tell me, he wasn't. Always
    excuses.

    SAVARKAR *turns, and is about to leave:*

GODSE. Stop! Wait!

    GODSE *takes his scissors, goes up to* KISHORE, *and holds
    them against his neck.*

APTE. What are you doing?

GODSE *drags him over to* SAVARKAR.

KISHORE. Tell him to let me go. Please! Don't do it –

KISHORE *sputters*.

GODSE (*to* SAVARKAR). I don't have to say the words.

(*To us*.) I thought I'd rise in his estimation. But that didn't happen.

(*Re:* KISHORE.) Oh he's okay. You okay? You want me to stitch this, Kaka?

KISHORE. I don't want to impose.

GODSE (*to us*). I had no inkling what was to come next.

3.12

SAVARKAR. I'm a free man now. Free as an Indian. My release was negotiated by the Congress leaders. Godse, I'm returning home next week.

GODSE. That's wonderful!

SAVARKAR. I'm going back to Bombay. After twenty-six years.

Pause.

KISHORE. You could move to Bombay too.

GODSE. Yes. I'll pack right away.

SAVARKAR. Do I look like I have his umbilical cord in my pocket? (*To* GODSE.). It's time to go on your own. What you and Apte do now is up to you. I hope it's more than just sewing blouses.

SAVARKAR *leaves*.

GODSE (*to us*). He left me without looking back. I'd made this town the centre of my world. I gave my life and soul to the political organisations that Savarkar patronised. I thought we'd do great things together. But he just... left.

Lights on APTE.

APTE. We are free to follow our own path now. Quit tailoring. It's beneath you. Let's start a paper! We must spread Hindu-ness to every nook and cranny of the country. An independent Hindu India is close, my friend. I can sense it.

Our cause needs numbers. Lucky for us, we are the majority!

They titter.

No more Ratnagiri, Godse. Our destiny is elsewhere.

GODSE. Our cause needed a militia's touch.We turned to Germany for inspiration. We procured firearms and ammunitions so our people could travel safely to Muslim areas, we led religious processions through Muslim streets to teach them a lesson, we enlisted young men as foot soldiers so our Hindu-ness could grow from strength to strength. Godse-Apte, the protectors of the Hindu way of life!

End of Act Three.

ACT FOUR

4.1

GODSE (*to us*). It's 1945. Britain may have won the World War, but it is at a great economic cost. India now holds the upper hand. We are on the cusp of independence now. We should be rejoicing, right? Wrong. Because of him –

Lights on JINNAH.

JINNAH. I don't believe that my people will be safe in a Hindu-majority country. Muslims have never had a voice in a Hindu-dominant region. We've never felt welcome here. We're made to feel as interlopers in a land that we've been living in for centuries. All these years, we believed that this region was a single homogeneous entity before the British. We were wrong. Just look at how frequently Hindu-Muslim clashes are occurring.

GODSE. Sadly I am not in charge. They are.

Lights on GANDHI.

JINNAH (*to* GANDHI). There is only one solution: Two separate dominions. A Hindustan for Hindus. And a Pakistan for us.

GANDHI. Impossible. What you are suggesting is to separate two brothers living in the same house.

GODSE (*to us*). He said that and immediately arranged to have more talks with Jinnah.

NEHRU *and* PATEL *now join* JINNAH *and* GANDHI, *and we move seamlessly to…*

4.2

...The same room, a different time. It's 1946. Delhi.

GANDHI. * You will vivisect my country over my dead body.
  We've coexisted for centuries. Our diversity has been our
  strength all these ages.

JINNAH. Has it, really? * We neither inter-marry nor inter-dine.
  Our concepts of life and death are different. Our epics and
  histories are different. The hero of one is the villain of the
  other. The victory of one is the defeat of the other. We are
  each other's natural enemy.

GODSE (*to us*). The word 'partition' has entered our
  vocabulary now. Because of that bloody Jinnah!

GANDHI. We are all human beings!

JINNAH. You and I shared the same vision once, but it was
  a fool's dream, Mr Gandhi. No more. We must have our
  separate sovereign nation when the British leave the Raj.

GANDHI. Let's not make rash decisions, from which we cannot
  return. You know as well as I, creating two nations will
  create two sets of problems rather than solving one. (*Looking
  at* NEHRU *and* PATEL.) Perhaps there's a way to
  compromise?

GODSE (*to* GANDHI). Come on! We already compromised
  when you agreed to meet him. No more. They're the
  minority. Is their turn to bend a little.

NEHRU. Jinnah saab. I assure you we'll be fair to every single
  citizen of undivided India. You'll have to trust us.

  JINNAH *laughs*.

JINNAH. Trust, Mr Nehru, when you've unilaterally rejected
  a federal structure that we'd already agreed on? We've been
  through this a million times. I've told you, I fear for my
  people in Hindustan. We'd only be switching masters from
  the British to Hindus.

GANDHI. We can all be masters in one nation. How can we calm your fears? Tell us. What would it take? Perhaps a Muslim prime minister of independent India?

JINNAH. Can a Muslim be a prime minister of independent India?

GODSE (*to* GANDHI). Tell him, absolutely not!

GANDHI. Absolutely, yes.

GODSE (*to* GANDHI). What the – Are you out of your mind?

JINNAH. Perhaps my friends from the Indian National Congress have a different opinion.

GANDHI. They are all with me. (*To* PATEL *and* NEHRU.) Aren't you?

Silence.

Nehru?

Pause.

NEHRU. We need to take into consideration what the majority feels about this, Bapu. We are being born as a democracy, the primary tenet of which is that people choose their leader.

JINNAH. This is my point exactly. How can we be represented fairly if we are the minority?

PATEL. Bapu, there is already a general feeling that we are ceding far too much to Jinnah saab –

GANDHI. It's not concession. It's safeguarding our people. If there are two nations instead of one, blood will flow through the streets.

PATEL. It will flow regardless.

JINNAH. No birth is possible without blood, Mr Gandhi. Look at it this way. In Pakistan, we'll be the majority.

JINNAH *exits.*

Silence.

GANDHI. You could give him what he needs.

PATEL. Oh, will the masses accept him, do you think? I'm
sorry, Bapu, but you are wrong in this instance. With him as
prime minister, our divisions will only deepen. He'll be
overseeing a further splintering of India.

NEHRU. The signs are everywhere, Partition is inevitable. It's
like cutting off the head to get rid of the headache, but Jinnah
has left us with no choice.

GANDHI. No choice? No choice? You are choosing not to see
the choice –

PATEL. We've been heading towards this conclusion for a
while now. This time, one man can't stop it. We've moved
past that. Let him have Pakistan –

NEHRU. Yes.

PATEL. At least we will have a unified India.

GANDHI *collects his things angrily.*

GANDHI. I can see you all had made up your minds even
before this meeting.

PATEL. Where are you going, Bapu?

GANDHI. Everywhere. We're about to unleash a catastrophe.
I have to appeal to people's buried humanity now.

NEHRU. Mountbatten has assured us a smooth transition. No
bloodshed or riots, he has promised.

GANDHI. Mountbatten has been here a few weeks! He doesn't
know a thing about us!

Lights down on NEHRU *and* PATEL. *As lights go slowly
down on* GANDHI…

GODSE (*to us*). No protests. No fast unto death, his favourite
form of blackmail – oh no no, that's reserved for the Hindus,
so that we'd bend to his will. Just like that, he accepted
Partition, he allowed a piece of our land to be given to them!
If peace had been that important between Hindus and

Muslims, we could have enforced it! Hindus had the numbers! But no one cared. Not Gandhi. Not the Congress. Not Mountbatten, who was hell-bent on a hard Brexit. You think that's funny? Think of the human cost! You send a man with little interest in my country to oversee Partition. You give him time till June 1948. What does he do? He advances the event by ten months. Ten months! So he can get the hell out of here! Then you hire another man called Radcliffe who'd never been to India and give him five weeks to draw the map for the two new countries. Did he, like a fucking child, draw a random line across the map? Is that how we became two countries? Yes, I blame Gandhi for all of this. If he hadn't harped on peace at all cost, if he hadn't given Jinnah a place at the table, if he hadn't been the one negotiating.

4.3

14th/15th August 1947. Two flags are hoisted – Pakistan's by JINNAH, *seventy-one, and India's by* NEHRU, *fifty-eight. Two sets of crowd cheer.*

One man sits alone and desolate, in mourning – GANDHI.

Two men sit on the terrace watching the fireworks – GODSE *and* APTE. APTE *is drinking.* GODSE *is like a coiled spring.*

RADIO. After a hundred and ninety years, British rule in India has finally ended. At the stroke of midnight of August 14th–15th, 1947, two nations were born – India and Pakistan. There was jubilation everywhere in the two newest countries as the Viceroy of British India, Lord Mountbatten, officially handed over the reins of the region to the Governor General of Independent Pakistan, Mohammad Ali Jinnah, and to the Prime Minister of Independent India, Jawaharlal Nehru.

JINNAH *raises Pakistan's flag.*

CROWD 1. Pakistan Zindabad!

NEHRU *raises India's flag.*

CROWD 2. Hindustan Zindabad!

Dancing, music, etc.

GANDHI *goes to bed, a desolate man.*

More fireworks burst. GODSE *snatches* APTE*'s bottle and smashes it to the ground in frustrated fury.*

CROWD 1. Pakistan Zindabad!

CROWD 2. Hindustan Zindabad!

GODSE *weeps.* APTE *tries to comfort him.*

4.4

GODSE (*to us*). And just as feared by all, except Mountbatten and the British government, the human tragedy that ensued was unprecedented.

GANDHI *is with survivors.*

1. Our own neighbours set our house on fire. For decades we'd lived together in peace. Overnight everything changed –

2. They abducted and raped and slaughtered all our women. I lost my wife, my mother, my children –

GODSE (*to us*). Two million Hindus, Sikhs and Muslims massacred on both sides.

3. I saw with my own eyes women with their breasts, noses, ears and cheeks cut off.

GODSE (*to us*). That's more than the entire population of Northern Ireland now.

4. They ripped the unborn babies from our women's bellies. No woman survived –

5. They shot at our train. All those sitting on the roof and in the compartments were killed. I rolled myself and my children in blankets we hid under our seats –

GODSE (*to us*). Close to fifteen million people were displaced on both sides of the border during the greatest and biggest exodus in human history. People poured in from all directions. Some refugee columns were at least fifty miles long.

GODSE *and* APTE *are with some* REFUGEES *in their office*.

6. I am from a small village now in Pakistan. All the Hindus and Sikhs collectively decided to migrate to India. I reached India safely, but the others, they were attacked by mobs. Out of the five hundred in that refugee column, only forty survived. My father lived because he lay on the ground, as still as the dead body next to him.

7. We took our belongings, all that we could carry, some cows, clothes, what little money we had, and we left our village. We walked night and day to Pakistan. Many could not stand the strain. We had to leave them behind. We never saw them again. Murdered. In cold blood.

GODSE (*to us*). Almost every single political issue in the subcontinent can be traced to this one event. Border skirmishes. Nuclear arms race. Kashmir.

1. We used to always talk about poetry and art, but that night I saw him come at me with a machete –

2. We sent our children ahead of us, we hoped they'd be safe from the carnage, we were wrong –

3. They've burnt down our villages. They've taken over our homes. We've nowhere to go.

GODSE (*to us*). Do you see what I see now? The bloody handprint of Gandhi in all of this.

GANDHI. I appeal to both nations, stop this madness, stop the violence. I beg you, we cannot allow colonial divisions to fester within us even after we are free.

4.5

GODSE (*to us*). Then came the last straw... Kashmir.

January 1948. PATEL *and* NEHRU *in their office*.

NEHRU. Bapu is going on another fast unto death, as we feared.

PATEL. What does he want now?

GODSE. The independent kingdom of Kashmir is under attack – (*To us*.) January 1948. We have stop Pakistan –

NEHRU. Release the five hundred and fifty million rupees we owe to Pakistan.

PATEL. What?

NEHRU. I know, I know. He's asking us to be patient.

GODSE. He's asking Hindus to be patient! He's asking India to be patient!

PATEL. Does he even realise – time is of the essence, Nehruji. We need military action and now.

NEHRU. He thinks he's weaving two nations together –

PATEL. Well, impossible. India's national interests are our top priority now.

NEHRU. Who is to tell him that? What if we release the five hundred and fifty million rupees as he wishes?

GODSE. No, no, don't even think about it –

PATEL. We lose what little edge we have over Pakistan. We lose Kashmir.

GODSE. Exactly!

NEHRU. If we don't release the money...

GODSE (*to us*). He dies.

PATEL. Yes.

GODSE (*to* NEHRU). Let him.

NEHRU (*to* PATEL). India needs Gandhi. If he dies, we lose our guiding voice.

PATEL. If he dies, we lose public support. We'll have our first elections soon, Nehruji. We need his goodwill. (*Pause*.) We need Gandhi.

GODSE (*to us*). No! This is going to be a pattern, Gandhi constantly undermining India in order to please Muslims.

Lights down on NEHRU *and* PATEL. *Lights up on* APTE.

APTE. Are you thinking what I'm thinking?

GODSE. Absolutely.

I couldn't stop Partition. But him, I can.

APTE. Godse, it's going to be the both of us as always.

GODSE. No, Apte. It has to be me. I've been preparing myself for this moment my entire life.

4.6

30th January 1948. Birla House garden. GANDHI *on his way to the prayer meeting.* GODSE *accosts him.*

GODSE (*to us*). January 30th. (*To* GANDHI.) Pranam, Bapu. May I have a moment?

GANDHI. Later, my child. I'm already late for the prayer meeting.

GODSE. Stop!

GODSE *pulls out a gun. Time freezes.*

Your prayers are of no use now. Your only scheduled event now is meeting your maker. You, sir, are no patriot. Mohandas Gandhi. You acted over and beyond your remit. I hereby find you guilty of high treason –

GANDHI *laughs*.

GANDHI. What high treason?

GODSE. You're once again lobbying for them, as if you're their father –

GANDHI. Them? Do you mean Pakistan?

GODSE. You know perfectly well what I mean!

GANDHI. Or Muslims?

Beat.

GODSE. Is there a difference? You have turned your back on your country and it's my duty –

GANDHI. Country. The people are my country. Perhaps you're referring to geographies that are hardly half a year old.

GODSE. Enough of your your pedantics! I have found you culpable and am sentencing you to death –

GANDHI *laughs again*.

Stop it! Stop laughing!

GANDHI. Or what? You'll shoot? Go ahead. I'm ready. I've been ready for my maker for decades, but perhaps he's ready now too. Why are you doing this, Nathuram?

GODSE. I just told you –

GANDHI. Half-truth! You are here, about to pull the trigger, Nathuram. I demand to know why.

GODSE. I don't have to tell you any damn thing – no, in fact I will tell you – Your ahimsa is bullshit, do you hear me? It is like a goddamn entrance exam – only a few can qualify and win the grand prize, your goddamn approval! Like you're some – fucking saint! No one can live up to your high expectations. Not even your own son could –

GANDHI. Yes, he was like you, hot-headed, rash –

GODSE. He doesn't even speak to you any more.

GANDHI. That was his choice, not mine.

GODSE. No, he sought your love and approval and you denied them to him! What sort of a father does that to his son?

GANDHI. So you're killing me because I'm a bad father –

GODSE *moves his gun closer to* GANDHI.

I'm only trying to understand you, my son –

GODSE. No! Don't call me son! I am killing you because, because, ahimsa, it's poison, should be destroyed –

GANDHI. Why?

GODSE. Because you've made my country weak!

GANDHI. Still chasing lies, Nathuram.

GODSE. It's the truth –

GODSE *tries to pull the trigger, but cannot as his hands tremble badly.*

GANDHI. Son –

GODSE. Don't. Say. That. Word –

GANDHI *watches as* GODSE *tries to calm his trembling hands.*

GANDHI. Even the pulling of the trigger requires a calm mind and a steady heart. Your himsa requires my ahimsa. (*Laughs.*) Nathuram, put down the gun. You are no murderer –

GODSE. I am! You know why? Because you made me one! You pretend to be this perfect father to all of us, but you're just a terrible father, you too have your favourites. Some of us can never be favourite children, no matter what they do, no matter how much they give up! You abandoned me when I needed you most!

GANDHI. It was you who abandoned everyone. Your family, your friends. Your goddess, me. You fail and then you blame us. But that's still not the real reason, is it?

GODSE. What the hell do you know about me?

GANDHI. Enough to understand that ahimsa is not the right path for you, you who dodges personal responsibility all the time, like a coward –

GODSE *presses the gun to* GANDHI*'s flesh.*

GODSE. Shut up! Shut up!

GANDHI. Always running away –

GODSE. Stop it!

GANDHI. Never having the fortitude to face your darkness – or the truth –

GODSE. The truth, old man, is it's all your fault! Yes. You made me. You, sir, are why I'm like this.

GANDHI. Like what?

GODSE. Like… this –

GANDHI. Like what, for God's sake – say it –

GODSE. Ordinary! You made me ordinary! I was destined to be somebody – but you made me like everyone else. I don't change lives, I don't make ripples… I don't matter.

Silence. GODSE *is appalled at himself.*

GANDHI. Ah, my son.

GODSE. My name is Nathuram Godse and I am not your son!

GODSE *shoots* GANDHI. GANDHI *falls.* GODSE *drops the gun, lifts up his hands and turns around. Time unfreezes.*

4.7

1949. GODSE *and* APTE *are in their respective cells.*

RADIO. The prime accused, Mr Godse and Mr Apte, have been found guilty of the murder of the father of our nation, Mahatma Gandhi, and have been sentenced to death by hanging. Mr Savarkar has been exonerated due to lack of evidence.

Lights on KISHEN *and* DAULAT.

KISHEN. Tell them how the country reacted to the verdict, bhai.

DAULAT. Celebrations all over. Fireworks. Sweets being distributed. The works.

KISHEN. Any sign of violence?

DAULAT. No bhai. Patel-saab has been very efficient with the policing. Extremist right-wing groups are being quietly disbanded as we speak. The criminals' act of hatred has in fact brought Hindus and Muslims together.

KISHEN. So there is no sign of... I don't know, a revolution?

DAULAT. Only in my bicycle, bhai.

KISHEN *and* DAULAT *laugh.*

APTE. Don't listen to them, Nathuram. The future will realise the truth and know that we killed for the country.

KISHEN. You killed for other reasons. No one had heard of Nathuram Godse before you killed Gandhiji. Now you've ensured your name went down in history along with that great man. But here is the thing. You will always remain a footnote. (*To* APTE.) And you, a footnote to a footnote.

DAULAT. How many of your friends have visited you in jail? None.

KISHEN. I was at the court the other day. I saw you trying hard to catch Savarkar's eye. But he never once looked at you, did he? Even your mentor has abandoned you.

DAULAT. Oh, did you kill Gandhiji to please Savarkar?

KISHEN. This is your fate. To be alone, reviled and insignificant. In life and death.

GODSE*'s fallibility hits him now.*

GODSE (*to us*). They are idiots. What the hell do they know? Revolutions take time to gestate. Weeks, years. Perhaps even decades. Right?

4.8

1949. Jail. AAI *and* BABA *have come to visit.* DAULAT *and* KISHEN *are on guard. Long awkward silence between* GODSE *and his parents.*

GODSE. If you're going to be silent, you may have as well not come.

BABA. We used false names. We booked our tickets under another name. We've not been able to use our real names.

Pause.

GODSE. Is everyone alright?

BABA. What do you think? Our son to be hanged for the murder of the most beloved man in the country.

GODSE. You should be proud of me. Your son is about to become a martyr.

BABA. Your name, our name will be synonymous with evil. I thought I'd raised my son better than this.

GODSE. Son, Baba? You, should be garlanding me in pride the way you used to when I was a child. Temples will be built in my name, your name. Think about that.

AAI. We should have let you be, as a baby. Whether you lived or died, we should have just left you to Fate.

Pause.

GODSE. I will be hanged tomorrow. Someone from the government will hand my ashes over to you. I have a specific request. I want my ashes to be immersed in the holy Indus river only in a unified Hindustan. I shall patiently wait for that day. However long it takes.

BABA *and* AAI *leave before above speech ends.*

4.9

KISHEN. It's time to go.

APTE *is also brought out of his cell by* DAULAT. GODSE *and* APTE *walk quietly. The two face two nooses.*

APTE. We did the right thing.

GODSE. We are heroes.

APTE. We get a good death.

GODSE. We get the perfect death.

APTE. For our Motherland.

GODSE. For our Hindu nation. Long live –

APTE. Undivided India!

Pause.

GODSE. My friend…

APTE. My Nathuram…

APTE *and* GODSE *hug.* APTE *is led away.*

Akhand Bharat Amar Rahe!

GODSE *steps into the noose.*

GANDHI *enters.* GODSE *turns.*

GANDHI. Oh, I am dead. You killed me.

GODSE. And you me. We are the cause of each other's death now.

You are gone and that's all that matters! I have erased you!

GANDHI. Yet here I am. Here, now, with them. What you seek to kill and bury loves to grow from the rubble. Like a jasmine vine. (*Smells the air.*) Do you not smell it?

GODSE. What I smell is gunpowder. Or is that hell?

GANDHI. What you think is hatred is actually fear. What is seized under fear can be retained for only as long as the fear lasts. One day, people will lose fear, then all the bullets in the world won't matter. What will you do with your hatred then?

GODSE. Oooh. I'm shaking in my boots. (*Re: us.*) Look at them! They're here for me.

GANDHI. Are they?

GODSE. It's better to be a Godse than a Gandhi. That is the truth. (*To us.*) We have to be ready. No, you have to be ready. Know who your enemies are. They are hidden amongst you. Your neighbours, your colleagues. You'll know. They don't speak your language, they don't share your values, they don't look like you. Strike them before they strike you. Cross over the yard and tear down their house first. Neutralise the threat before it grows into a monster – no, obliterate them. Your enemies are getting stronger, bloodthirstier. Your future, your place in the world is at stake. What will you do? A Gandhi is of no use to you when tomorrow's battles are fought with deadlier weapons. No, you'll need a Godse. And I will rise.

Blackout.

Curtain.

www.nickhernbooks.co.uk

facebook.com/nickhernbooks

twitter.com/nickhernbooks